CON...
the darkness

word for **TODAY**

CONFRONTING
the darkness

Colossians: Christ the supreme power

JOHN GRAYSTON

SCRIPTURE UNION
130 CITY ROAD, LONDON EC1V 2NJ

© John Grayston 1994

First published 1994

ISBN 0 86201 770 X

British Library Cataloguing-in-Publication Data.
A catalogue record for this book is available from the British Library.

Unless otherwise specified, Scripture quotations in this publication
are from the Holy Bible, New International Version, Copyright ©
1973, 1978, 1984 International Bible Society, published by Hodder
and Stoughton.

Phototypeset by Intype, London.

Printed and bound in Great Britain by Cox and Wyman Ltd,
Reading.

To Jenny
without whom
confronting the darkness
would have been so much harder

ACKNOWLEDGEMENTS

No book is the product of one person and this is no exception. I should in the first place acknowledge my debt to previous commentators, especially J B Lightfoot, Ralph Martin, P T O'Brien, F F Bruce and Dick Lucas. Also to those who have influenced me over the years and without whom my faith would not be what it is today.

Thanks to Becky Totterdell, who not only commissioned the manuscript but was kind enough to read and comment constructively, despite having moved to a new job. The task of picking things up mid-way went to Alison Barr whose judicious changes have produced a host of improvements. Thanks, too, to Tony Hobbs for his comments and to Emma Bliss and Penny Boshoff for the finishing touches. The trouble with mentioning names is, of course, that the list becomes endless and one is tempted to say paraphrasing the writer of Hebrews, What shall I say? I do not have time to tell of production staff, designers and the many others without whom the book would not have been possible.

I must, however, express particular thanks to Michael Green for permission to quote from Person to Person, and for the time he put in to amend the spoken word into a suitable form for print.

CONTENTS

INTRODUCTION

Gathering for worship on a beach in Tuscany one evening I was impressed by the thought that the sea, whose waves were breaking gently on the beach, was the same sea that Paul had travelled nearly 2000 years earlier. There was a sense of the years rolling away. His work and ours were one, his problems and ours so similar. Though the world has changed in ways that go far beyond anything that Paul could have imagined, the message he proclaimed and lived has real meaning for us today.

Four hundred years before Paul's time, Colossae was a large and important city. Situated on the river Lycus (now the Curuk-se) in Asia Minor (modern Turkey), it was located in a fertile area known for its large crops of figs and olives, and was a prosperous city, deriving its income from the wool trade. By Paul's time the city was in steep decline. The neighbouring cities of Laodicea and Hierapolis had expanded and taken some of the prosperity from Colossae. One scholar has said that 'Colossae was the least important city to which any epistle of St. Paul is addressed.'

It lay on a key route between Greece and Rome in the West and the older empires of Persia in the East. In the first century the majority of the population were either local inhabitants or Greek settlers. There appear to have been small Jewish settlements in the area some 300 years before Christ, and in 61 BC when the Roman governor, Flaccus, seized the Jewish Temple tax we know by the sum this amounted to that there were around 11,000 adult Jewish males. In Colossae Roman thinking, Egyptian ideas, Greek philosophy, Jewish religion, and primitive superstition were all mixed in a way that was typical of the first century. Our world is just as diverse.

Paul is writing to a church he never visited. His route to Ephesus may have taken him through the Lycus valley but it is more likely that he went further north. In any case it is clear that he was not responsible for the evangelisation of the area and did not know the churches personally (2:1). When Paul worked in Ephesus (around AD 54–57), however, his team were active in church planting in the outlying towns, and it seems that the Epaphras of whom Paul speaks so warmly in 1:7, 8; 4:12, 13 was responsible for bringing the good news to Colossae. Most of the church were probably Gentile Christians but there are references which suggest that some were converted Jews.

We cannot be certain when Paul wrote the letter. He is in prison and we know of only two definite imprisonments – Caesarea (Acts 23:23–25) and Rome

(Acts 28:16, 30, 31). There is also an early tradition that he was imprisoned in Ephesus, an imprisonment which may be hinted at in 1 Corinthians 15:32 and 2 Corinthians 1:8. The two most likely places and times for the writing of Colossians are Ephesus sometime during the years AD 54–57 or Rome around AD 60–61.

Whatever its date, it is clear that by the time of the letter the Colossians are having problems with false teaching. The exact nature of this has been debated but it seems likely to have been a mix of the ideas which flourished in the ancient world – some from the East, others with roots in Judaism, or the old Greek and Roman religions. These ideas, supplemented by primitive superstition, science and occult practice, made a heady concoction with wide appeal.

The Colossians were therefore, working out their faith amidst a ferment of religious ideas, against a background of social change and economic decline. Their immediate world was one of relative political stability, but Colossae was situated at the edge of the Roman empire and dark forces lay beyond creating ill-defined but real fears. In many ways their situation was remarkably similar to our own. Paul's letter to the Colossians is a word for us today.

The Colossians were suffering from more than just false teaching. Though there was much about the life of the church for which Paul could give thanks – the people's grace, love and fruitfulness (1:3–8) – there were also things that distressed him. The Colossian church was just like any other church. I remember visiting one some years ago that had a great reputation. It was respected for the quality of the preaching, its zealous outreach and its enormous range of activities. Talking to some of the members gave a different picture. The church was divided into factions; some people never spoke to others. Not surprisingly, many experienced a sense of death rather than a sense of life in the worship! When we see a church that is flourishing, where God appears to be at work, we assume that all is well. It fits our definition of a successful church. Paul saw things differently. He rejoiced in what he saw God doing but gave time and energy to working and praying for continued growth and change.

We cannot see exactly what was going wrong in Colossae. Paul's letters are often like one end of a telephone conversation. We hear his response and have to do some detective work to understand what is happening at the other end. Whatever our conclusions we can be sure that there will be lessons for us. For our world has parallels with the world of the Colossians: our church life with theirs.

PART 1
CHRIST
AND THE
WORLD

1
WHO'S IN CHARGE?

Acid rain, holes in the ozone layer, earthquakes in Armenia. These, to say nothing of famine in Somalia and Mozambique and war in Bosnia and Cambodia, are the stuff of which newscasts are made. Meanwhile malaria kills thousands and a new drug resistant strain of TB, a disease once believed to have been eradicated, sweeps the world.

It is not surprising that people ask again and again, 'If God exists and he is powerful and he is a God of love, why. . . ?' I have heard it from fifteen year-olds whose main concern is their street cred and I have heard it from a veteran of the trenches of the Somme. To many people the Universe looks like a giant practical joke. Or a runaway truck careering down the hill out of control.

Whose world?

The Colossians would have struggled with the question of 'why' too. Many would have blamed their gods for disasters. But their gods fought and squabbled among themselves – they were weak, mean and selfish. Modern men and women have no such imperfect gods to blame. For us the 'why' remains a puzzle. Paul's answer is to point his readers, then and now, to Christ. His supremacy is the great motif which runs through the whole letter, the common strand which draws all others together, and provides us with two of the greatest descriptions of the risen Lord in the New Testament. The chaos is real enough but it is not permanent or final. There is a hand on the controls:

> He is the image of the invisible God, the firstborn over all creation. For by him all things were created: things in heaven and on earth, visible and invisible, whether thrones or powers or rulers or authorities; all things were created by him and for him. He is before all things, and in him all things hold together. And he is the head of the body, the church; he is the beginning and the firstborn from among the dead, so that in everything he might have the supremacy. For God was pleased to have all his fulness dwell in him, and through him to reconcile to himself all things, whether things on earth or things in heaven, by making peace through his blood, shed on the cross.
>
> *Colossians 1:15–20*

Every moment of every day we are aware of the world around us. The air we breathe, the food we eat, the people we meet, our own bodies – all are frequent reminders that we are part of something bigger. The birds that wake us (well, some of us!) in the morning, the flowers, the trees, the sea or the mountains that we escape to on our holidays – all are integral to the created order.

The world is both a beautiful and a hostile place. For this reason people at other times and in other places have given trees, rivers and mountains spiritual significance. They, or the spirits which live in them or are identified with them, are worshipped or feared. The Bible gives a different picture. Its doctrine of creation is a simple one, beautifully stated in the opening chapters of Genesis. In the beginning there was God. He created the heavens and the earth from nothing. He simply spoke his word and the world as we know it came into being. When the Hebrew in which the Old Testament was written talks of a word, it talks of something that is active and creative, that when spoken achieves something. When operation Desert Storm began and troops moved in to relieve Kuwait from Iraqi occupation, fearsome firepower was released by one word from the generals. What power is released by the word of God! When he speaks things happen.

The world and everything in it was made by God. Trees, rivers and mountains are not to be worshipped in themselves. Like the sun and the moon, calm and storm, their purpose is to bear witness to God (see Genesis 1; Psalms 19:4; 29; 104; 107–29). Jesus takes up a similar thought when he speaks of God feeding the birds and clothing the flowers (Matthew 6:25–30). The emphasis is on a God who provides for his people, giving them all they need. When the people of Jesus' day looked at the world around them and at the food on their tables, they saw evidence of a great and loving God.

This simple yet profound view of the universe has been accepted in the Jewish and Christian worlds for over 3000 years. But no more. One of the best-selling books in recent years has been Stephen Hawkings' *A Brief History of Time*. In it the author portrays a Universe without a Creator. In 1992 Richard Dawkins presented the Royal Institution Christmas lectures, arguing for a thorough-going evolutionary approach to the world which left no place for God. He has since said that God is a computer virus of the mind.

These are simply two examples of a wider trend. Let's say we no longer believe in a Creator. The universe was the result of some big bang; billions of year ago, worlds formed and gradually, out of the primeval soup, life emerged. Primitive life forms increased in complexity, emerged from the water, and continued to increase in complexity until finally we ended up with the state of affairs we know. None of this can be finally proved, at least in detail, and there is certainly sufficient doubt for us to maintain a healthy scepticism. But what is particularly alarming is that millions of intelligent people find it easier to believe that all this happened in some chance way than to accept that God was involved. What claims to be scientific fact is, in some ways, just as much an expression of faith as belief in a Creator God! Science, too, operates within a framework of beliefs which cannot be proved. This is not the place to discuss the mechanics of creation in detail, but it is vital for the Christian to hold on to the fact that God made the world and that it was a good world.

What's gone wrong?

If God made such a good world how come we have ended up in the mess we're in? The story of Genesis tells us that the human desire to do things our own way rather than God's way introduced the problem. I recently acquired a new piece of Bible software for my computer. Anxious to view the results I loaded the programme. I did not, of course, read the instructions – I knew what I was doing! Not only did I have the programme loaded incorrectly, but I managed to corrupt some other files and had to spend a couple of hours sorting things out. This is rather like what has happened to the world. When Adam and Eve chose to do things their way, they began to go badly wrong. When Frank Sinatra sings, 'I did it my way. . .' he is simply reflecting the spirit of human beings who want to do without God.

Human beings have gone their own way all through history but the results have become increasingly obvious. In the eighteenth century the Industrial Revolution caused a major change in the way people lived. People moved to towns and cities and lost the close awareness of natural rhythms that goes with living off the land. God became more remote. Production had to increase. Coal and iron were mined. Coal was burned in ever increasing quantities followed by gas and oil in various forms. The atmosphere gradually filled with one pollutant after another. The result is all too clear. Gasses in the atmosphere have created the so-called greenhouse effect, and the world is gradually getting warmer, leading to unpredictable changes in climate and vegetation. (Those who think that global warming will enable them to enjoy a Mediterranean winter in the Shetlands or on the shores of the Hudson Bay may be in for a rude awakening – and they have forgotten that thousands will be drowned as the Polar ice caps melt.) Holes are appearing in the protective layer of ozone (in February 1993 at its lowest level since records began over Europe) causing an increase in skin cancer and damage to vegetation. In part at least, this frightening scenario is a consequence of losing sight of the Creator who gave the world to men and women to look after for him. As we struggle with the doubts and fears that uncertainty over the future brings, it is good to learn from Paul that Christ is still in control. This is a positive message to offer our fellows. Faced with a world apparently adrift, the Big Bang theory offers little hope, and evolution small comfort. But the knowledge that there is a Creator caring for our planet is something worth holding on to.

Who cares?

Human response to the plight of the planet has been mixed. Some people carry on regardless. Others believe that Science, the god of the twentieth century, will find us a way out of the mess – a strange conviction as it was the worship of this rather demanding god that got us into the mess in the first place! Increasingly, however, many share a desire to care for the world and ensure that something is preserved for future generations.

Christians should be at the forefront of such initiatives. Unfortunately, this isn't always the case. Too often we leave the field to others. A number of green groups have appeared, many consisting of sane and thoughtful people whose approach is based on sound scientific principles. Others have adopted basic principles which owe more to a woolly paganism. We hear talk of mother earth, of the earth mother or earth goddess, and the Gaia theories of James Lovelock have met with widespread appeal. But though these had their origin in solid scientific research, presented more 'popularly', they make the earth into a knowing, feeling being. It becomes an organism with an independent, self-contained life of its own. There is nothing new in this; the Greek philosopher Plato put forward such a view 600 years before Christ, and Paul would have met people who shared his thinking. Paul wants to make it clear, however, that the earth derives its life from God himself. Day by day it is sustained by his influence. Without his power it would collapse. We care for it because God made it and wants us to treat it responsibly, not because it has some personal soul at its heart.

Controlled by the stars?

In Britain at the start of 1992 no less than four of the popular daily newspapers made their main selling pitch their special horoscope supplements, containing detailed predictions for the coming year. Millions of people consult their horoscopes in daily papers or weekly magazines. They listen to astrologers on breakfast television. There is a growing sale of books with detailed horoscopes. There are horoscope phone-in lines.

It is generally assumed that no one takes any of this seriously. But in that case why bother to read or listen in? In fact there can be no doubt that for some people the stars are exceedingly important. Some American and European companies apparently consult astrologers before making business decisions. Nancy Reagan is believed to have consulted an astrologer while her husband was President of the United States and it has been suggested that she may have influenced some of his decisions as a result. All this demonstrates that the veneer of civilisation is wearing thin. Paganism is not so far beneath the surface. Once people stop believing in God anything goes.

In 2:8 and 2:20 Paul refers to the basic principles of this world (NIV). In Greek philosophical thought the *stoichea* had come to mean the basic elements which made up the world – earth, fire, water and air. Some of these elements, most notably air, were seen to possess life-giving forces and spiritual qualities. It is an easy step to believe that the upper air and those bodies which it was thought to contain were in some way divine. Hence the underlying principle of astrology that our lives are under the control of stars and other heavenly bodies. This idea seems to have been embraced in part by some in the church in Colossae.

The true Christian response is clear. When other things take the place that belongs to God, and we start to follow their guidance, problems follow. Our world is full of idols – not in the sense of objects of wood or stone but in the sense of human ideas and ideals. Here in Colossians Paul goes to the root of the problem. Why should we worship created things when we can worship the Creator? We don't look at a Constable, a Gainsborough or a Monet and talk about the genius of the painting without appreciating far more the genius of the painter.

We respond to creation in a similar way. A night sky pin-pointed with light, a sunset with its range of subtle tonal variations, the intricacy of a daisy, the splendour of a snow-capped mountain range – all these and so much more enable us to exclaim with the writer of the hymn,

Then sings my soul my Saviour God to Thee,
How great Thou art, How great Thou art.

Who's at the hub?

The false teaching in Colossae that we discussed earlier diminished Jesus. Paul's response places Christ firmly back at the centre. All false doctrine undermines the person and the role of Jesus. The answer is always to come back to him. And if we start by seeing him as the One through whom God brought the entire universe into being, we shall have the beginning of a correct perspective.

Jesus Christ has existed from eternity with the Father in the Godhead. Only if this is true could he have been involved in creation. We cannot accept a Christ who is anything less than fully and eternally God. These verses (Colossians 1:15, 20) stand against any attempt to reduce his status. Whenever we see this happening – whether by Jehovah's Witnesses or New Agers – we can be sure that something is wrong.

Any attempt to worship beings other than Jesus Christ seems thoroughly stupid. And when we look at all that he has done for us, what can we do but respond in worship?

As creation is the work of Christ it follows that it is good and that we should value it. In chapter 2 there are indications that the false teaching in Colossae made a great deal of obeying rules about fasting. Its followers probably had a fairly low opinion of the world. They would have taken on board some of the Greek thinking which saw the world as essentially evil, with the human soul trapped in a body. The only way of dealing with the world and releasing the soul to fulfil its true destiny was to suppress all that belonged to the body and to the evil material world. Now, there is an important truth here. We do need to deal with the wrong desires which drag us down. But to say they come from the body and the physical world while all good and wholesome desires come from the soul is misleading.

It is still possible to find Christians who think that the world is evil and to be avoided, although I meet fewer these days than I did twenty years ago. This is a view that needs to be challenged. The world as God created it through Jesus is good. It has been marred by human sin but it is still good: the hand of God is in it. We can joyfully and thankfully accept the world and all that it contains, including much that is the creation of men and women. We can affirm our culture, our art, our society as being part of a good world gone wrong rather than as part of a completely bad world. We need to be careful about the things that we condemn – we might be condemning things that Jesus has placed in his world. The image of God can still be found in human creativity and human love even when it is difficult to recognise. This is not to say that we should accept everything without thinking. We shall return to this subject later in the book. For the present let us learn to view the world positively.

Above all, let's catch the force of Paul's argument in this passage. He wants us to see the powerful Christ, creating the world and holding it together and, as we do so, to determine to follow him and him alone. We realise as we bow before him that any rivals are weak and tawdry, that beside him they pale into insignificance. Any false gods, be they the angelic powers of the Colossians or the materialistic idols of twentieth-century western society, fade before the supreme power and glory of the creator Christ.

> *Jesus is Lord, creation's voice proclaims it,*
> *For by his power, each tree and flower was planned*
> *and made, Jesus is Lord, the universe declares it,*
> *Sun moon and stars in heaven cry Jesus is Lord.*

2
WHERE'S THE REAL POWER?

A few years ago I was with Scripture Union colleagues in Jamaica. They had been sent a new van which was sitting in the docks. All they had to do was go and pick it up. Except that the docks wouldn't release it without evidence that it had been taxed. So off to the licensing authority; who couldn't tax it until it was insured. Fine, only no one would insure it until it was in the country and that meant out of the docks. It took one of my colleagues two days of standing in queues to gain possession of that van!

More recently my son was trying to explain to the local Council why he did not feel he should pay the full Community Charge for the ten-week period between leaving school and starting college. 'You have to pay,' was the response, 'you weren't a student for those weeks.'

'Fine,' he replied. 'In that case I'll claim Housing Benefit.'

'No, you can't do that. You were a student and students aren't eligible.'

A brick wall. Feelings of complete powerlessness.

These are two fairly trivial examples of a common problem. Individuals come against the system and find that they cannot make any progress. The rules say something and that's the end of the matter. The decision of some clerk behind a desk is final and there's no court of appeal. This sense of frustration can be found everywhere but it particularly affects the weak and the vulnerable.

Governments act in our name and there is little we can do. Even in democracies where we have some power through the ballot box our influence is strictly limited. A recent newspaper advert asked, 'Shouldn't the system give us what we want not tell us what we want?' This sums up the feelings of many people.

Company boards make decisions which affect the lives of thousands of people. In order to make greater profits they decide to sell products to countries in the two-thirds world which are not needed and which may even have harmful consequences (baby milk and pharmaceuticals are two recent examples that spring to mind). Nearer to home factories are closed down throwing hundreds out of work and creating untold misery. Now, there are no simple solutions to most economic difficulties, but the effect of actions such as these is to leave us with a feeling that there are powers which determine the course of our lives and over which we have no control.

The worst demonstrations of this apparent loss of control are the enormous cruelties of war to be witnessed on our TV screens night after night or in the smaller scale tragedies which have equally devastating personal consequences. Some years ago I was with a group of colleagues from around the world. One went off to phone home and returned with the news that a friend of his teenage daughter had been taken out and shot – a not uncommon event in his country. Day after day hundreds of street children in the cities of South America quietly disappear, hunted and killed like vermin. Again and again individuals feel powerless in the face of forces they cannot control.

Something nasty in the woodshed

What is it that gives power to some and denies it to others? What is it that makes normal people act in strange ways when given authority or placed in a uniform? History shows us that human structures can take on a life of their own. Many of those who were caught up in the evils of Nazism were sensible, rational human beings. Those who looted on the streets of Los Angeles in May 1992 were normally law-abiding citizens. Those who control big businesses don't set out to create economic problems for the poor of the world. Governments may pass laws with the aim of creating good conditions for the bulk of their citizens and yet the result may leave many feeling powerless and oppressed. Looking at the world it is very hard to avoid the conclusion that somehow evil has worked its way to the very heart of our institutions.

Two verses in Colossians give us a clue to understanding the root of the problem:

For by him all things were created: things in heaven

and on earth, visible and invisible, whether thrones
or powers or rulers or authorities; all things were
created by him and for him.   *Colossians 1:16*

... having cancelled the written code, with its
regulations, that was against us and that stood
opposed to us; he took it away, nailing it to the cross.
And having disarmed the powers and authorities,
he made a public spectacle of them, triumphing over
them by the cross.   *Colossians 2:14, 15*

At first sight all this seems rather strange. Paul talks of
beings whom we cannot see but who nevertheless are
very real. This is not some primitive world view that
we can ignore at will but, the Bible says, the truth. For
most of history no one has questioned the existence of
spiritual beings. In many parts of the world today it is
only by believing in their power that people can make
sense of the world as they find it. But the idea of invisible
beings doesn't exactly appeal to modern humanity in
the West. It smacks of primitive superstition. We believe
we now understand things scientifically and do not need
this talk of spiritual powers.

Paul described these beings in words that his
readers would have understood. Jewish and Greek
thought worked with a common terminology. The
words are not exclusively religious ones – indeed they
have their origin in political and military contexts. They
all indicate a degree of power, control or authority.
Possibly they refer to several levels of authority among
the spiritual beings. The verses from chapter 2 suggest
that these invisible beings, or some of them at least, are
actually hostile to the human race. Whether good or

evil, however, Paul wants us to know that even the most powerful are no match for Christ.

Evil pervades human structures and the New Testament is aware of this. The book of Revelation was written against the background of a state machine that was doing all it could to destroy the life of the church. When John talks of Babylon he describes a bloodthirsty power which is given over to evil, and the world has seen many such in the centuries since. He also talks of economic powers who oppress the poor – selling men and women as though they were mere commodities (Revelation 18).

Some modern readers have therefore assumed that when Paul speaks of principalities and powers he is only talking of the structures of society – for us today, governments, civil authorities, corporate institutions, the armed forces, Trade Unions. But both his language and his world view are more in line with an interpretation in terms of spiritual forces. Such forces may well influence the structures of society – indeed all the evidence suggests that they do, and it should not surprise us that they operate in this way. Disruption is an especially effective weapon in their struggle to oppose God and mess up his creation. The injustice and oppression we see are evidence of this activity.

Evil at large

Talk of demons, or of such a thing as a personal devil, causes problems for many modern readers, at least at one level. Until a few years ago, the whole idea would have been treated with scorn – something for primitive people in other parts of the world. Things have changed.

Many Christians in Europe and America have become more aware of the power and presence of evil forces. Some too much so! Others are still uncertain about what to make of the idea. For the early church the issue was quite clear cut. The power of evil was very real in the ancient world. Many of the Christians in Colossae had been converted from a situation in which they had lived in constant fear of the powers of demons. And even as Christians they still wondered whether demons had power over them. Given the concern that many Christians have about the influence of demonic forces in their lives, and the increasing number of people specialising in deliverance ministry, the issue is still a live one.

Twenty or so years ago we used to pride ourselves on our sophistication. Twentieth-century humanity had come of age. It no longer feared demons nor did it worship God. But something strange has happened. A string of 'supernatural' thrillers from the pen of Stephen King and others, a wealth of films of the same nature and we are faced with a gullible public, who are ready to believe almost anything. The words attributed to G K Chesterton sum it up: 'when people stop believing in God they do not believe in nothing they believe in anything'.

We have seen an explosion of interest in the occult. This ranges from the supposedly harmless glance at the horosocope in the morning paper, through to Satanism. Reports of the ritual abuse of children may have been somewhat exaggerated and are notoriously difficult to prove, but clearly there is something nasty lurking in the shadows. The people we work with, travel with, study with, possibly even worship with may, unknown to us, be involved in some of these activities.

Dabbling with these occult things looks interesting, but it can have devastating results. School children playing with Ouija boards or experimenting in other ways have found unexpected and frightening things happening and a number have become disturbed as a result.

An obsession with horror films can in some cases lead to depression and suicide. On Hallowe'en 1992 the BBC showed a fictional drama about haunting and possession which took the form of a current affairs type of investigation. A number of people took it as fact, and there is still some doubt as to whether the advance publicity made the true nature of the programme clear. One father blamed the effects of the programme for the death of his son. Why do these things happen? In some cases, of course, we are dealing with impressionable people, and what we witness is the result of their own instability. But in other cases there is evidence of something more. The interest and the activity has opened the way for evil to gain a foothold in the mind and the imagination. Increasingly those of us involved in pastoral work are meeting those who have been affected in some way.

The effects will not always be the same; sometimes there will be obvious and frightening signs as with the man Jesus met among the tombs of Gerasa (Mark 5:1–20). At other times there will be very little. I remember talking with a man who was trying to justify leaving his wife and setting up home with another woman. He told me how this was a good Christian thing to do. There was some suggestion that he had been involved to a small extent with spiritualism and

Eastern religions. Whatever the case he was consciously preferring darkness to light. Evil had completely distorted his way of thinking, but he remained calm, rational and perfectly controlled.

Captives

Freedom is one of the great slogans of the twentieth century. I spent many of my teenage years in Malawi, then Nyasaland. Towards the end of my family's time there pressure was increasing for independence and I remember vividly driving through a group of stone-throwing demonstrators and hearing the shout 'Kwaca', freedom.

Many protest movements in other parts of the world have had their roots in the same desire for freedom. Recently, we have seen the collapse of the Berlin wall and considerable changes in the map of Europe. We want to be free and not dictated to by others. Young people do not want to be told what to do. Employees want a say in how companies are run. And none of this is wrong.

Yet freedom is often something of an illusion. Sometimes all we do is to exchange one form of captivity for another. The revolution that rids us of the tyrant only gives power to another. This is another mark of the influence on our lives of the powers.

Our captivity to the powers can take many forms. It is most obvious in the addictions that individuals have to drugs or alcohol but many are held in captivity to other obsessions or patterns of behaviour. Some are trapped by the attitudes or actions of others. Most of us lack, in one way or another, the complete freedom to become the people we want to be. Paul's language reflects this:

> See to it that no-one takes you captive through hollow and deceptive philosophy, which depends on human tradition and the basic principles of this world rather than on Christ.   *Colossians 2:8*

When he talks of the powers being disarmed it implies that they have power over us until they are disarmed. Often in his other letters he talks of the freedom that God gives through Jesus.

Victory from the jaws of death

Although spiritual beings have real power, it is not absolute power. Jesus made them and therefore he has the final authority. He is superior to them in every way. But, as we have just seen, some spiritual beings have rebelled and have created havoc. Jesus came to bring them to heel. . .

> . . . having cancelled the written code, with its regulations, that was against us and that stood opposed to us; he took it away, nailing it to the cross. And having disarmed the powers and authorities, he made a public spectacle of them, triumphing over them by the cross.   *Colossians 2:14, 15*

The cross spelt final defeat for the rebellious powers. All those who had been held captive are now freed. The writer of Hebrews puts it like this:

> Since the children have flesh and blood, he too shared

in their humanity so that by his death he might
destroy him who holds the power of death – that is,
the devil – and free those who all their lives were
held in slavery by their fear of death.

Hebrews 2:14, 15

It is often thought that the place of victory is the empty
tomb. But both these passages point to the cross. In
order to understand what is going on here we should
take a closer look at the life of Jesus. Right from the
start there is a battle. Herod sets out to destroy the baby
Jesus (Matthew 2:16–18). And after his baptism,
when Jesus goes out into the wilderness to prepare
himself for his ministry, what is the result? A time of
great spiritual blessing? Not exactly. More a period
of fierce battle and temptation. This sets the tone for
his ministry (Matthew 4:1–11). Time and time again he
is confronted with demonic forces who oppose him.
One revealing incident occurs early on:

> Just then a man in their synagogue who was
> possessed by an evil spirit cried out, 'What do you
> want with us, Jesus of Nazareth? Have you come to
> destroy us? I know who you are – the Holy One of
> God!' 'Be quiet!' said Jesus sternly. 'Come out of
> him!' The evil spirit shook the man violently and
> came out of him with a shriek.   *Mark 1:23–26*

This struggle takes place every time Jesus is confronted
by those with demons. It takes place when he is confronted by the sick. It takes place when he is opposed
by the authorities. All of his life Jesus was battling with
the powers of evil.

The struggle climaxes at the cross. In the Garden

of Gethsemane Jesus prays, prays desperately, that the cup might pass. In other words that another way might be found. But there is no other way. And so he goes to the cross, bearing the sin of the world, to do final battle with the originator of that sin. At the cross love triumphs over hate, light drives back the darkness and where Satan once reigned Jesus now reigns supreme. We can look back to the cross with a great sense of relief. The Jesus who came to set the captives free (Luke 4:18) has now done just that.

All this should make us wary of taking the power of evil too lightly. If Jesus was caught up in battle we can expect to be caught up too. The enemy may be defeated but pockets of resistance remain. We should be warned against the sort of triumphalism which assumes that victory is automatic or even easy. For us, as for Jesus, there will be struggle and pain. For us there will also be times of failure as well as times of success.

Warfare on the streets

In recent years an increasing number of Christians have taken to the streets in praise marches. The picture which Paul uses in Colossians 2 is remarkably similar. When he talks of the powers being led captive in Christ's victory processions he is thinking of the victorious Roman general coming back into Rome after a successful campaign. He would ride in on his chariot, followed by the army and then, in chains, the captives from the defeated enemy. The enemy was seen to be routed. Victory was publicly proclaimed and demonstrated. There was no doubt as to who had won. The praise march works in a similar way, by declaring in public that Christ won the victory at the cross. This was a public event for all to see and the church is called to demonstrate that victory publicly in many ways. We shall look at others later in this book.

For some these praise marches are simply a way of proclaiming Christ. Others look on them as a way of confronting evil powers, believing that there are demonic spirits who rule over geographical areas and that by going out in the name of Jesus such territories can be reclaimed for him. There is some biblical support for this idea but it is limited. The most obvious reference to spiritual powers having control of a specific area is in Daniel 10:13.

> But the prince of the Persian kingdom resisted me twenty-one days. Then Michael, one of the chief princes, came to help me, because I was detained there with the king of Persia.

The most natural way to understand Daniel's reference to the Prince of Persia is as a human leader. But the reference to Michael, later called 'your prince, Michael', seems to suggest some sort of angelic power. Certainly later Jewish thought saw Michael as a powerful angelic being (see Jude 1:9; Revelation 12:7). It seems reasonable therefore to regard the Prince of Persia as a spiritual power who has some control over Persia. If this is right, then there is a battle going on in the heavenly places which is reflected in some way in the battle taking place on earth.

This sort of thinking has been popularised in Frank Perretti's books, *This Present Darkness* and *Piercing the Darkness*. For Perretti, the battle which rages between angelic beings and demons is affected by the actions of his human characters. Perretti emphasises that his books are fiction not theology and he might be disturbed to see the extent to which they are sometimes quoted as apparently authoritative source books on spiritual warfare. But what they have helped to do is to put spiritual warfare back on the agenda. For too long the church has behaved as if the supernatural does not exist. We have discovered to our cost that it is only too real and we don't always know how to cope with it; we certainly can't cope with it in our own strength. Jesus is the victorious one. The powers know that they are defeated and that their power is gone. We do not need to win the victory; it has already been won. This is why we need to be careful about the language that we use. We often pray (or some of us do) that the 'evil one might be bound'. Fine, so long as we realise that he is already bound and that all we are doing is proclaiming the victory of Calvary. But if we somehow think that our prayers are going to have the effect of binding Satan, we are placing too much reliance on ourselves and not enough on the finished work of the cross – and that is the way to disaster.

Through his victory, Jesus has authority over the powers. In practice, however, the spiritual battle is, as has been suggested – and as we find in practice – very real. The Devil is described as the Accuser. He is spoken of as a roaring lion who goes about looking for people to devour. For us to be aware of the dangers that we face and the resources available to us is wise. The weapons God has provided for us are beautifully described in the well-known passage in Paul's letter to the Ephesians:

> For our struggle is not against flesh and blood, but against the rulers, against the authorities, against the powers of this dark world and against the spiritual forces of evil in the heavenly realms. Therefore put on the full armour of God, so that when the day of evil comes, you may be able to stand your ground, and after you have done everything, to stand. Stand firm then, with the belt of truth buckled round your waist, with the breast-plate of righteousness in place, and with your feet fitted with the readiness that comes from the gospel of peace. In addition to all this, take up the shield of faith, with which you can extinguish all the flaming arrows of the evil one. Take the helmet of salvation and the sword of the Spirit, which is the word of God. And pray in the spirit on all occasions with all kinds of prayers and requests. With this in mind, be alert and always keep on praying for all the saints. *Ephesians 6:12–19*

Not much doubt here about the nature of the conflict. Some of the terms are the same – 'authorities', 'powers' – but others are new – 'spiritual forces'. The overall impact is similar: we struggle. The word is a strong one implying that the Christian life is not always easy. The struggle is not against human powers – although they may well be involved – but against spiritual ones. Paul bases his description on the armour of a Roman soldier – possibly even the one who was standing guard over him as he wrote.

This armour is our safeguard in the struggle. Because the stock-in-trade of the powers are lies and deception (John 8:44), our weapons include truth. Living in a world where so much cannot be trusted,

Christians should be people of integrity. Whenever we show that truth matters we strike a blow at the powers. The need for righteousness may make us feel inadequate – after all we know how far short our behaviour so often falls. But righteousness is something that God gives us – we are put right with him, and nothing can change that. The enemy may often try to tell us that we have been deserted by God because of our failure but we know that God has promised never to abandon us. And as he gives us the strength to live in the right way, the power of evil is weakened.

We also, as we shall see later, have a message to tell. It is a message of peace. The forces of evil want to bring brokenness and hurt into the world. The Christian longs to bring wholeness and wellbeing – that is, peace. None of this can happen in our own strength. That is why Paul reminds us of the shield of faith. Ultimately it is trusting in God that will ensure that we are not defeated by evil. So we need to remind ourselves frequently that we trust in him. We need to remind ourselves too that he has saved us (the helmet of salvation), and that he will go on saving us.

Our sword is the word of God. When Jesus faced the Devil in the desert he responded three times to his lying temptations with the truth of the Bible (Matthew 4:3, 6, 10). If we are to make any strides forward in the battle we need to understand what the Bible says and be able to apply it to the situations we face. Supreme in all this is prayer. Spiritual warfare begins and ends in prayer; not in brief superficial prayer but in lives of prayer. God is always present with us and in us and we can relate every situation to that. We live in dependence on him and we call on his resources.

It would be nice to take a short cut around this. But we cannot. Spiritual warfare is hard work. We trust in the victory that has already been won, but we have to apply it in our own experience as we take these weapons for ourselves. And persistent prayer is the key.

The last word

How do we respond as Christians? We certainly don't want to fall into the trap of thinking that evil has no power or that demons don't exist. Equally we don't want to go to the extreme of finding demons lurking everywhere. They exist, they have real power but they are not the direct cause of all human illness or misfortune. There are some Christians who seem to live in fear of demonic powers. We need to be careful that we do not deny the victory of Jesus. The powers were crushed when Jesus went to the cross and they no longer have any final power over us; we can resist them in the name of Jesus, confident that they will have to give way. That does not mean that it will be easy. Often there will be a long struggle with temptation. Those who become Christians with a history of involvement in any occult activity may find that repeated prayer and ministry from others is necessary to bring about the final victory, and this is an area best handled by those with experience. There are too many stories of people who have been damaged by well-meaning but badly executed attempts to deal with problems of this sort. For those involved the important thing is to hold on to the victory of Jesus, to pray in his name, to read the Scriptures, to find others to pray with and ultimately to seek help from those with experience.

Paul's great purpose in Colossians is to show us that Jesus is superior to all these things because he made them and defeated them. For us that will mean that wherever we find the ravages of evil we can still trust in his ultimate power to bring about justice. This is not easy. To look at an individual with great potential, cruelly damaged by the presence of the demonic, to look at starving children in war-torn Somalia or Mozambique, to see the oppression of Christians in the old Eastern bloc or at the hands of the Shining Path in Peru – all of these things will test our faith.

Sometimes the victory will come through a change in circumstances. When Wilberforce fought against slavery he was standing in the name of Christian freedom against an evil which permeated the structures of his society. Profound change came as a result. Sometimes it will come through hope being expressed in the middle of hopeless situations. I have just had a letter from friends who regularly visit what was Yugoslavia. They quote a woman who escaped from Sarajevo with nothing: 'Two weeks ago we fled Sarajevo and lost everything. Here we found Jesus Christ. It makes it worth all the suffering we have been through.'

Sometimes there will be no obvious victory. The struggle will continue and evil may seem to be winning. At such times we hold on, knowing that the last word of history rests with the Lord Jesus Christ. He created all and it exists by his power to bring glory to the Father. He redeemed it all from the frustration to which sin had subjected it (Romans 8:20). He won a final victory over those who would tear it from him and he will return to reign in glory.

3
HOW
MANY
PATHS?

One of the major British news stories of the last few years has been the death threat against author Salman Rushdie on account of his book *The Satanic Verses*. The Islamic community in Britain reacted so strongly that the threats had to be taken seriously by the authorities – leading to considerable expense in the way of police protection – and by his publishers – who have still not produced a paperback version of the book. For many British people, acquainted with a fairly genteel form of Christianity, the sight of the Muslim community holding public protests and burning books in the street was all rather surprising.

During the same period there has been controversy over the purchase and conversion of a large mansion in Hertfordshire for use by the Transcendental Meditation group, which has roots in Indian Hinduism. Many towns in Britain, and in other parts of the Western world traditionally thought of as Christian, have

Muslim Mosques, Hindu Temples and Sikh Gurdwaras. The ideas of Buddhism appeal to many who are disillusioned by the pressures of modern life. We rub shoulders at school and at work with people from totally different religious traditions.

The religious smorgasbord

This religious diversity is a new phenomenon. Until the end of the Second World War Britain was relatively isolated. People of other faiths lived in other countries. They were heathen. We went with the truth and evangelised them! All relatively simple, if inaccurate. Now that we live in the same towns, attend the same schools, work alongside one another, life is much more complicated.

The nineties have been designated by the Christian church in the UK a Decade of Evangelism. This concept has aroused some hostility. There have been a number of protests from Jewish groups about Christian missionary endeavours. As other faiths protest about Christian attempts to evangelise, or in their view, proselytise, them, we tend to lose confidence and withdraw. Or we continue in ways that are insensitive and alienating. It is probably not going too far to say that there is a crisis of confidence in many parts of the contemporary church in regard to its evangelistic task.

To be fair this is not an entirely new problem. There have always been those, both from the Christian church and from the communities of other faiths, who have argued that different faiths are but different roads. The destination is the same. God is at the top of the one mountain and while different paths might start at different points and pursue different routes they will inevitably arrive at the same summit – for there can, of course, only be one summit.

Anyone who has done much walking on the hills will find this analogy unconvincing. There are all too many summits, one beyond the other, each offering false hope. Worse still, in some places if you arrive at the wrong summit your chances of reaching the one you were aiming for are remote. In the English Lake District, Scafell and Scafell Pike (the highest mountain in England) are adjacent peaks, part of the same massive outcrop. But mistake a path in your attempt to scale England's highest peak and end up on Scafell, and your way to Scafell Pike is blocked by a two hundred foot sheer drop. The journey can only be made by a round-about route involving considerable retracing of one's steps. This illustrates the fundamental truth that there is only one God and only one way to reach him.

In some ways our present great melting pot of religious notions takes us back into the world of the first century. It is possible that never since then have we known quite such a mix of ideas. Most years I make at least one trip across the English Channel and recently most of these have been on a ferry that is owned by a company with its roots in Scandinavia. One of the restaurants features a smorgasbord – the traditional Scandinavian buffet. The choice is frightening – several varieties of cold meat, cold fish, salads, bread, fruit, hot dishes. It is difficult to know where to start – and when to stop! To modern men and women the religious scene has much in common wth a smorgasbord. There is so much on offer. It doesn't really matter what you choose – it's simply a matter of personal taste. Paul's world was like this too. To him it represented a wonderful opportunity and a great challenge.

God's enemies

If we want to understand how Paul sees other religions we must stand back a little and see how he views those who don't know God:

> For God was pleased to have all his fulness dwell in him, and through him to reconcile to himself all things, whether things on earth or things in heaven, by making peace through his blood, shed on the cross. Once you were alienated from God and were enemies in your minds because of your evil behaviour.
> *Colossians 1:21–22*

Before they came to faith in Christ the Colossians were God's enemies. They were not simply neutral. Nor were they able to reach out towards God. They were totally alienated.

Into such situations comes the God who rescues and who reconciles. He builds bridges to alienated humanity. He draws together those who are at odds with one another. And he does it through the death of Jesus. The language is clear; all things are reconciled by Christ. He has made peace between humanity and God. All of us are outside God's kingdom, alienated from him, at enmity with him, imperfect, unholy, disqualified people. And the only way this situation can change is through the cross.

In case we should be in any doubt, Paul talks about us being dead:

> When you were dead in your sins and in the
> uncircumcision of your sinful nature, God made
> you alive with Christ.   *Colossians 2:13*

The picture may be different but the effect is the same.
One does not have a relationship with a corpse. And
that is how we appear to God until we are given new
life by Jesus.

We have here a clear statement that only Jesus can
deal with our separation from God. The good news
which he announced was freedom from the old domination and a new life in the Kingdom of God. The New
Testament does not give us any scope for seeing other
faiths on the same level as the truth which God has
revealed in Jesus.

A new direction

Paul hadn't always seen things this way. The first time
we meet him in the New Testament he is known as Saul
and is standing by at the killing of Stephen, one of the
early Christians. He then dashes around the country
making Christians' lives an absolute misery. But God
breaks in and on the road to Damascus Saul discovers
that, far from being God's friend, he is his enemy.

God has a purpose for Saul though. After meeting
Christ on the road to Damascus his whole life is given
over to telling others the good news. The scene shifts
to Damascus. God speaks to a man called Ananias,
'Go to Straight Street and see Saul.' Now Ananias was
no fool. He knew about Saul. This man was hounding
Christians. 'Go and pray with him?' he asks. God's
response is a simple one:

> This man is my chosen instrument to carry my name
> before the Gentiles and their kings and before the
> people of Israel.   *Acts 9:15*

This sense of divine call never left Paul. He knew that
God had met him and that his life was now determined
by the will of God and not by his own ideas. He had
no choice but to tell others – he was driven to do so by
the deep conviction that this was what God wanted of
him. That is why he starts his letter with the words,

> 'Paul, an apostle of Christ Jesus by the will of
> God. . .'

This is the clue to his whole life's purpose. The word
'apostle' comes from the Greek word meaning 'to send'.
An apostle is simply one who is sent. When the church
in Antioch (Acts 13:1–3) sent Paul and Barnabas off to
preach the good news they were recognising what God
had already done in the life of Paul.

The great divide

But there was more to it than that. Paul was also driven
by his experience of the love of God: 'For Christ's love
compels us, because we are convinced that one died for
all, and therefore all died' (2 Corinthians 5:14). He had
found something so good that he had to tell others
about it. This is why he continues his letter to the
Colossians:

> We always thank God, the Father of our Lord Jesus
> Christ, when we pray for you, because we have

> heard of your faith in Christ Jesus and of the love
> you have for all the saints... *Colossians 1:3, 4*

Paul says something like this in most of his letters. He rejoices when people become Christians. As Jesus does (Luke 15:7). And as we do too. There is excitement, satisfaction, a sense of wonder and so much more when we see others coming to faith. It is more than pleasure at someone joining our club – it is the recognition that God has brought change into someone's life. To have faith in Christ Jesus makes a difference. For Paul it is the key difference.

> ... giving thanks to the Father, who has qualified
> you to share in the inheritance of the saints in the
> kingdom of light. For he has rescued us from the
> dominion of darkness and brought us into the
> kingdom of the Son he loves, in whom we have
> redemption [through his blood], the forgiveness of
> sins. *Colossians 1:12–14*

I enjoy photography, and one of the subjects I had always wanted to photograph was an air-sea rescue. I don't really know why – perhaps for the obvious symbolism. One day a few years ago I was with my family on holiday in Wales. Standing on the cliffs, on a windy day, camera and telephoto lens in the bag, we noticed some people in canoes out to sea. They seemed to be struggling. Slowly, despite their efforts to come to land they moved further out to sea, the wind and the waves proving too strong for them as they became more exhausted. Then we heard the drone of a helicopter. It flew over the cliffs. It hovered over the canoes. A man was winched down, the occupants were winched up, the helicopter returned and they were safe. As the helicopter flew off into the distance I realised that the camera had remained untouched in the bag. The drama of the event had taken over. Obviously I don't have what it takes to make a good press photographer!

When we look at the rescue Jesus has achieved we will be similarly captivated. The idea of rescue brings to mind a picture of people who are helpless to do anything about their own condition until someone comes in from outside, someone who is stronger. We are left with the impression that apart from God's saving action there is no hope for men and women.

Paul talks about a complete change. We move from one kingdom into another, from darkness into light. Like someone leaving the horrors of an oppressive regime – like Terry Waite or John Macarthy emerging from years of captivity in a small dark room – we emerge into the daylight. We pass the border post and there is no going back.

Paul uses three other pictures here. He tells us that God has qualified us to share in his kingdom. When we apply for a job we need certain qualifications. The advert and the job description will tell us what they are. If we lack those qualifications our chances of getting the job are not great. There are qualifications for entering the kingdom of God – qualifications we cannot meet. Only when God provides the qualifications can we go in. Imagine you are off on the holiday of a lifetime. You leave the plane full of anticipation and excitement. But the immigration officer takes one look at your passport and says, 'You can't come in. You don't have a visa.' All your hopes are dashed. And then another official comes over and hands you a visa. You can pass through.

We shall return to the pictures of redemption and forgiveness in a later chapter. For the moment it is enough to note that they too are pictures of change.

Unravelling the mystery

For Paul the gospel comes as a final revelation.

> Now I rejoice in what was suffered for you, and I
> fill up in my flesh what is still lacking in regard to
> Christ's afflictions, for the sake of his body, which is
> the church. I have become its servant by the
> commission God gave me to present to you the word
> of God in its fulness – the mystery that has been kept
> hidden for ages and generations, but is now disclosed
> to the saints. To them God has chosen to make
> known among the Gentiles the glorious riches of this
> mystery, which is Christ in you, the hope of glory.
> We proclaim him, admonishing and teaching
> everyone with all wisdom, so that we may present
> everyone perfect in Christ. To this end I labour,
> struggling with all his energy, which so powerfully
> works in me.   *Colossians 1:24–29*

We shall look again at this passage in a later chapter when we discuss the church's mission. For the present, let's take a closer look at this word mystery. What does Paul mean? For us a mystery is something that we cannot explain or solve, something unknown. When Paul uses the Greek word *mysterion* he is thinking of something rather different.

In the first centuries there were any number of strange cults that claimed to have the final word from

God. Only those in the know had the secret. It was deliberately hidden from those who were not members. This gave a feeling of great importance to those who had been initiated. Interestingly there are parallels with our current situation, as our look at the New Age will show.

These groups attracted a significant following. One, which centred around the worship of the god Mithras and included some particularly gory rituals involving the killing of a bull, was especially popular in the Roman army. Others were more popular in specific localities or among particular social groups. The Roman authorities were quite happy to allow such groups their freedom as long as their worship did not interfere with official religious practices which by this time involved the worship of the Emperor and were an important means of achieving political unity.

Fully aware of all this Paul takes up the term 'mystery'. But he gives it a new meaning. For him the good news of Christ is not something hidden; it is something to be broadcast. Any hiddenness lay in the past, in the years of preparation. God had been moving towards this majestic climax in which his sublime purpose would suddenly be revealed. Like a painter working quietly in the studio on his great masterpiece God had been preparing for this point. And now the public are invited in to see the great work.

In the passage, Paul defines the mystery in two ways. It is the 'word of God in its fullness' and it is 'Christ in you'. All God's purposes for humanity are summed up in the coming into the world of his son. Revelation 13:8 talks of 'the lamb slain before the foundation of the world'. This is how far back the plan goes. We see hints of what God is doing throughout the Old Testament. The sacrificial system speaks of his way of dealing with human sin; the Passover lamb of deliverance through death. The prophets look forward to a suffering servant, to an anointed king, to a new covenant. In each of these ways God has spoken, but now at last he reveals himself through his son (Hebrews 1:1–3). This is the universal message of the Bible, that something final and distinctive has happened in Jesus.

The only hope

Hope is something we all need. But in our world it is in short supply. Too many people have become hopeless because they cannot find work or food, or because they are doomed to be perpetual refugees, drifting from one country to another. Night after night we see the faces of the hopeless on our television screens. If we look we will see them on the streets of our cities too.

When Paul talks of Christ in us as the hope of glory he is not thinking of one possible hope among many. He is looking at people who were once no-hopers, alienated and at odds with God, and saying that Christ is their hope. When we use the word hope we often mean something rather vague: 'I hope it will not rain.' The Bible uses the word in a much stronger way. The 'hope of glory' indicates something sure and certain. We will experience this glory. Glory belongs to God and we lose it when we lose touch with him. To have the hope of glory is to be assured that we have security with him, now and in the future.

The idea of glory also makes us take a closer look at what God has done for us in Christ. Why should

God operate in this way? Who knows, except that his actions stem from his whole nature which is love. They stem from his desire that men and women might live in relationship with him. He acts the way he does because there is no other way. We who are enemies can do nothing about bringing ourselves back; but God can and has done something. Hence the phrase 'the glorious riches' of this mystery. Here is hope for hopeless people – and here is the only hope for hopeless people.

There is something about this great plan that makes us stop in awe. We want to respond with love and worship. These are elements to hold on to. Faith should affect us at the level of our emotions, it is something to get excited about. Think again about the painter inviting the public in to see the finished masterpiece for the first time. Imagine the gasps of excitement, the expressions of pleasure, the silent admiration, the desire simply to stand and drink in the beauty; in the face of God's masterplan these are appropriate responses.

There is one other factor that we must look at before we try to summarise. In chapter 2 Paul wrestles with the false teaching that was creating such problems in Colossae.

> So then, just as you received Christ Jesus as Lord, continue to live in him, rooted and built up in him, strengthened in the faith as you were taught, and overflowing with thankfulness. See to it that no-one takes you captive through hollow and deceptive philosophy, which depends on human tradition and the basic principles of this world rather than on Christ. For in Christ all the fulness of the Deity lives in bodily form, and you have been given fulness in

Christ, who is the Head over every power and authority. In him you were also circumcised, in the putting off of the sinful nature, not with a circumcision done by the hands of men but with the circumcision done by Christ, having been buried with him in baptism and raised with him through your faith in the power of God, who raised him from the dead. When you were dead in your sins and in the uncircumcision of your sinful nature, God made you alive with Christ. He forgave us all our sins, having cancelled the written code, with its regulations, that was against us and that stood opposed to us; he took it away, nailing it to the cross. And having disarmed the powers and authorities, he made a public spectacle of them, triumphing over them by the cross. Therefore do not let anyone judge you by what you eat or drink, or with regard to a religious festival, a new moon celebration or a Sabbath day. These are a shadow of the things that were to come; the reality, however, is found in Christ. Do not let anyone who delights in false humility and the worship of angels disqualify you for the prize. Such a person goes into great detail about what he has seen, and his unspiritual mind puffs him up with idle notions. He has lost connection with the Head, from whom the whole body, supported and held together by its ligaments and sinews, grows as God causes it to grow. Since you died with Christ to the basic principles of this world, why, as though you still belonged to it, do you submit to its rules: 'Do not handle! Do not taste! Do not touch!'? These are all destined to perish with use, because they are based on human commands and teachings. Such regulations indeed have an appearance of wisdom, with their self-imposed worship, their false humility and their harsh

> treatment of the body, but they lack any value in restraining sensual indulgence. *Colossians 2:6–23*

Human or divine?

Paul contrasts the teaching which the Colossians were following with the good news about Jesus. One is seen as based on human traditions, the other on the power of God. Human traditions suggest an attempt to reach God. From men and women of early times bowing in front of trees to the more sophisticated ideas of other world faiths, there is evidence of a longing for something beyond. Augustine, bishop of Hippo in North Africa from AD 395 to AD 430, wrote, 'Our heart is restless and can find no rest until it finds its rest in you'; the modern evangelist may talk of all people having a 'God-shaped blank' in their lives – both point to the same reality. Much of the current interest in the supernatural and the occult reveals a deep longing for something beyond the material routine of daily existence.

There are many well-intentioned attempts to find God. But they all go astray at some point. Men and women were made in the image of God and in each of us there remains something of that image. We all, therefore, have some idea of who God is and what he is like. But our faculites have been twisted by the effects of sin on the human race. The gods that we construct for ourselves owe something to our dim recollection of our origins. They owe something to our observation of what the world that God made is like. But they also owe something to the perverted and perverting activity of evil. Human traditions have their value, but compared to the revelation of God in Christ they can never be any better than pale shadows.

The basic principles are the *stoichea* that we met in a previous chapter – the forces which control the world. Some of the false religion that was prevalent in Colossae owed its origin, not simply to warped human ideas, but to the direct activity of demonic forces. In 1 Corinthians Paul recognises that the idols to be found in the temples had no real existence – but that behind them were the spiritual beings we looked at in the last chapter.

This view formed the basis of the great missionary thrust of the Christian church in the eighteenth and nineteenth centuries. Those in other countries who followed different religious paths were described as heathen and were believed to be worshipping demons. It is easy to understand how this came about when one looks at the strange and contorted representations of God to be found in some places – a god who is vicious and lustful, petty and selfish. Many early missionaries felt a profound sense of evil as they stood in some temples. Sensitive Christians still do.

The idea that other faiths are primitive heathenism or completely demonic is no longer acceptable. People from these faiths are understandably offended by such accusations. The charge is often demonstrably untrue for there is much that is good and worthy to be found in their teaching and their lifestyle. Paul himself was prepared to build on what he found in other religions, and to quote from their traditions. His evangelistic methods involved debate as well as preaching.

Relating to others

Where, then, does that leave us? How do we work out the implications of living in our multi-faith society in ways that reflect both our understanding of the unique place of Jesus and our concern to be fair and loving to our neighbours?

We need to have respect for others. Paul had a great love for his fellow Jews (Romans 9:1–3). He respected the philosophy of the Athenians (Acts 17:16–34). Nowhere do we find him being critical or writing off the religious convictions of others. His criticism is reserved for those who claim to be Christians but who live inconsistently. We shall want to understand others and affirm what we can in their culture and beliefs. We shall want to meet them as equals and discuss with them our own beliefs. We shall want to listen as well as talk.

We cannot do so in a vacuum, however. The fact that we shall listen sensitively and accept that God can and does speak to and through those who are not Christians does not mean that we must view all faiths as equal. As we have seen the Bible does make unique claims about Jesus. It regards him as the ultimate revelation. When Paul in Colossians talks about him being supreme, it means he is just that. This is not negotiable.

If we believe that Jesus is the only way to God then we shall want others to enter into relationship with him. This is the basis for Paul's drive. He simply would not have understood the problems we have about whether we should or should not evangelise certain groups. He certainly took the good news to Jews and to those who worshipped the Roman and Greek gods, believing that they were wrong and that God had spoken in Christ. These ideas are not particulary congenial today. Clifford Longley, discussing the problem in an article in *The Times* (August 17, 1987) points to the tensions between our concern for the salvation of others and the need for good relationships. He concludes that the dangers of seeing all religions as equal is that religion itself ceases to be important:

> ... everyone has to pretend that one religion is as good as another, and by implication that religion does not really matter.

At the same time he recognises that:

> What the new communities of faiths in Britain have in common is that they reject such indifference, and do indeed regard religion as important, and their own religion as true, the others as false. They must be puzzled by the attitude of the churches here.

Perhaps we have to rediscover our confidence in the truth of what we believe and practise while recognising that the credit for this does not go to us. God has revealed the mystery; we have not unearthed it by our own efforts. This should keep us humble and prevent us from speaking to others in ways that leave them feeling devalued.

Whatever turns you on

I once sat next to a man on a plane who, it became clear as we started to talk, was a fairly hard-bitten engineer. Within the first five minutes of conversation he said, 'I never discuss religion or politics.' This seemed to be a fairly clear warning. It was going to be difficult, I thought, explaining to him that I was a Christian publisher. His response was a fairly typical one. 'If that's your thing, then go ahead, but don't bother me with it.' Confronted with the smorgasbord of religions, people see faith as a personal matter. They may think us a little strange, but if we keep our faith to ourselves then we are just harmless eccentrics.

Somehow we have to insist that our faith is not simply a personal, private matter. It is about those great truths by which we live our lives, by which the universe is governed, by which we can know a relationship with God. These are truths which everyone has the right to hear and to respond to – not simply as our ideas but as God's truth. I have no right to ram anything down other people's throats, but nor do I have any right to keep it rammed down mine!

There are many things that we can do alongside people of other faiths. We can work together on issues of social justice, although we shall frequently find that in these areas we do not have full agreement. Islam and Hinduism, for example, do not value human life in quite the same way that Christianity does, although our practical record has not always borne out our convictions. We can work with people of other faiths on issues of environmental concern. Often we will find that they have a greater awareness of the physical world than we do and a greater concern for it. We can even stand with them on the need for spiritual values in a world which can rarely see beyond the material.

We can also discuss with them. In a multi-faith society we need to know and understand one another's convictions. We need to see where God may have been at work in their traditions and be able to acknowledge what is good. Our society can only function when there is respect across faiths. Christians should have nothing to do with the war that springs from religious differences. Winston Churchill is reputed to have said that, 'Jaw, jaw is better than war, war.' This is true in the religious realm too. There are many incidents in our history that we have cause to be ashamed of. The treatment of Jewish people by those who have claimed to be acting in the name of Christ has been appalling. The Crusades have consequences for Christian-Muslim relations even today, 600 years later. The New Testament doesn't give us any mandate for making war on people just because they have different beliefs – and it certainly never sees war as a way of bringing them to faith. Discussion, however, is a different matter. Paul was happy to debate, indeed it seems to have been one of his favourite evangelistic methods. Christianity will stand up in debate – we need not be afraid of getting involved in it.

We cannot, however, worship together. Many prayers from other traditions are beautiful and capture a real spirit of devotion. Every time we use a Psalm we are using the prayers of another religious tradition, albeit one from which Christianity grew. We could find prayers from other sources that we could gladly make our own. But to stand side by side in a common act of worship is to pretend that serious differences do not exist. It is to assume that all paths are equally true. It is to deny that Christ is supreme. Multi-faith worship may recognise our common humanity and need for the divine. But at best it involves giving glory to human traditions and at worst it means the worship of spiritual beings other than God – the powers of the last chapter. Paul would have nothing of that!

We should attempt to explain our own convictions. Other faiths require men and women to earn their right to a relationship with God. They leave people in bondage to a set of rules or to fear. Jesus came to break the bonds. Through him God offers a way back that depends solely on what he himself has done. People who live in bondage have a right to know this truth and to make their own response.

But we should tell them sensitiviely. Too often we have shown little respect for other faiths and their followers, and that is no way to reflect the love of God. To build on the basis of existing understanding is far more effective. We shall have to understand something of the beliefs of those we want to reach. Paul took the trouble to find out what he was up against. The preaching of the New Testament addressed to Jews reflects their faith. The preaching to Greeks shows an understanding of their way of life. This does not mean that we shall always agree with those we are trying to understand. Sometimes there will be a need to challenge, but first we must build a base of friendship and respect. We need to understand the context in which we are working and to find the most appropriate bridge. Then we may be heard.

In all of this we can retain our confidence in what God has done in Christ. There need be no diffidence, no timidity. God has spoken. God has acted. What he has done in giving his own Son is so amazing that we can shout it from the rooftops without any need to apologise. Our longing, like that of God, is that all might see Jesus as supreme.

4

THE
CRYSTAL
MAZE

As I write a previously unknown village in the West of England is firmly in the news. A large number of so-called New Age travellers, supplemented by middle-class ravers, has descended on the common next to the village. In the eyes of the villagers they are creating a nuisance. In the eyes of the travellers they are simply having a good time. But why New Age? Are these travellers genuinely a mark of the New Age? What is it anyway? And how should the Christian respond?

This book is not the place to answer all these questions. But in Colossae Paul faced problems that have a great deal in common with the ideas that we find in New Age thinking, and in our attempts to confront the New Age today we can learn from Paul's approach. It soon becomes apparent that the so-called New Age is not particularly New (nor for that matter is it an Age, but let that pass). It isn't one set of ideas. It is rather a strange mix of Eastern religious thought, alternative medicine, occult practice, old fashioned paganism, green philosophy, and a good deal more. Take, for example, this report on Totnes, normally thought of as a quiet town in Devon:

> Along with the Gestalt therapists, biodynamic massagers, the Shiatsuists, the nutritional councillors, aromatherapists, hypnotherapists, Tantra trainers, Reiki practitioners, Tibetan monks, Indian mystics, retreaters and would be students, come people disillusioned and dispossessed as if to Lourdes, Ladakh or Benares. There is a feeling of spiritual renaissance in the air.
>
> *The Independent, 21 May 1992*

This gives a good flavour of the New Age atmosphere. Much of it is a reaction to the ways of thinking that came in with the Enlightenment and the Industrial Revolution, that everything has to be explained, leaving no room for mystery, that everything has to be seen in terms of the material, leaving no room for the spiritual.

Searching for truth

The New Age reflects an increasing sense of disillusionment with this sort of thinking and with the modern world. Philosophers have not brought us the sense of well-being and wholeness that we crave. Science has not given us perfect health. The machine age has given us many labour-saving devices, but even more weapons of mass destruction. Politics has brought neither economic success nor good relationships in society. People are lonely, isolated, lacking any meaningful sense of their place in the order of things.

Influenced by an old astrological calendar the theory goes that we are about to leave this age, the age of Pisces, and enter the New Age, the Age of Aquarius in which the spiritual takes over from the material, community from individuality. Previous ages, so the theory goes, have led to fragmentation and breakdown, but the New Age brings truth and enlightenment and togetherness. There is nothing new about this. Back in the second century there was a group called the Gnostics. They, like New Agers, were not a tightly-knit group but a collection of different groups with different ideas. The word Gnostic comes from the Greek word *gnosis*, meaning knowledge. They were the people who had the truth, the knowledge that would guarantee salvation. Some have thought that the false teaching in Colossae was a form of Gnosticism. This is far from certain, for there is little evidence of Gnostic groups this early. But there are similarities and perhaps common roots. Against this background Paul claims that the truth is really found in the gospel:

> . . . the faith and love that spring from the hope that is stored up for you in heaven and that you have already heard about in the word of truth, the gospel that has come to you. All over the world this gospel is bearing fruit and growing, just as it has been doing among you since the day you heard it and understood God's grace in all its truth.
>
> *Colossians 1:5, 6*

There will always be other claims to truth. We have seen that in our chapter on other religions. But the Christian conviction is clear – God has spoken in Christ.

Son of God or cosmic Christ

Not all New Agers would deny this. Some talk of Christ in ways that seem almost Christian – speaking of Christ living in us. But look deeper and their understanding of Christ is quite different to that of Christian belief. New Agers think in terms of a cosmic 'Christ spirit' which inhabits all people to a certain degree – and some to a much greater degree. They talk of us becoming Christs for ourselves. Paul's response to this sort of thinking can be deduced from a passage with which we are becoming familiar:

> He is the image of the invisible God, the firstborn over all creation. For by him all things were created: things in heaven and on earth, visible and invisible, whether thrones or powers or rulers or authorities; all things were created by him and for him. He is before all things, and in him all things hold together. And he is the head of the body, the church; he is the beginning and the firstborn from among the dead, so that in everything he might have the supremacy. For God was pleased to have all his fulness dwell in him, and through him to reconcile to himself all things, whether things on earth or things in heaven, by making peacethrough his blood, shed on the cross. Once you were alienated from God and were enemies in your minds because of your evil behaviour. But now he has reconciled you by Christ's physical body through death to present you holy in his sight, without blemish and free from accusation – if you continue in your faith. *Colossians 1:15–23*

Jesus, as we have already seen, exists in his own right. We have seen him as Creator of the universe, but in going back to these verses again we see a deeper truth. Here is one of the clearest descriptions of the eternal relationship between the Father and the Son. The two have always existed, and when Jesus comes to this earth it is not as a human who has received a special measure of the Christ Spirit – it is as the eternal Son of God coming among us as a man.

The Jesus who came to this earth was not God loosely disguised. He was not some first century manifestation of the universal Christ Spirit who can also be found in Buddha, the Hindu gods, or any one of us who finds the right way. We have seen how he was present at Creation and how all things were not only made by him but are kept going by him. Impersonal spirits do not create things; this Son of God possesses all the qualities of personality as we know it. He also possesses all the qualities of God. Long before the world was he lived in relationship with God the Father. And when he came into the world it was to show us exactly what the Father was like. In the face of modern theories which reduce Christ, or God, for that matter to the level of vague impersonal spirit or force ('may the force be with you'!), we need to emphasise that God is a person with whom we can have a personal relationship.

In his response to those who claimed to have the truth, Paul does not resort to abstract arguments; he takes us back to a person. This is important. At the heart of our faith is not a list of things we must believe but a relationship. We are unlikely to convince anyone by argument and we shall certainly not make much impact on those who prefer New Age principles. But introduce someone to a Person and you are on their wavelength. One of the great mistakes in the history of the Church has been to reduce Christianity to a system of belief. It is no wonder lonely people have preferred the New Age.

The search for experience

The New Age offers a great variety of experience. Soothing massage with essential oils, lying in a warm tank of water in the dark, applying crystals to various points on the body to release new energies, listening to channelled messages from spirit beings. You pay your money and you take your choice (and it will cost you – the other day I found a leaflet on my car offering me half an hour of aromatherapy for £28).

The New Age represents the ultimate search for experience. But the truth is that the New Testament offers us one experience so satisfying that we will not need to turn to another tomorrow. It offers us, as we have seen, an intimate relationship with God, Christ in us in a very different way to that offered by the New Age. God comes to take up residence in those who love him. This is one of the most wonderful and comforting things about our faith. God also transforms our character so that it reflects his own as he has shown it to us in Jesus (Romans 8:29).

Some strands of New Age thinking suggest that we all become gods for ourselves. Now, as we have just seen, we do share in God's nature and character, only in him do we realise our true potential. This is the exact opposite of New Age thinking where the emphasis is on relying on the resources within ourselves. Humanity has now reached a point on the evolutionary scale where we can realise much more of the potential buried within us than we could when we were weak people dependent on God. The great New Age discovery is simply the old lie from the Garden: 'Eat and you will become like God' (Genesis 3:3–5). In other words, 'You don't need God. You can manage perfectly well on your own!' The independence which drives us away from God is at the root of our downfall. The Greeks had a word *hubris* which translates roughly as the sort of independent pride which, in the English proverb, 'comes before a fall'.

The fact is that we don't like to be dependent on other people. It makes us feel inadequate. And we don't want to be dependent on God. In chapter 3 we spoke about 'man come of age'. Modern men and women have grown up. They do not need God. God was a great idea for primitive, non-scientific humanity, but he is quite unnecessary for modern sophisticated individuals of the twentieth century – a prop to be discarded. However for men and women to live without God is much the same as a fish trying to live out of water. When Paul quoted the Greek poet to the effect that, 'in him we live and move and have our being' (Acts 17:28) he touched on the fundamental truth. We can only truly fulfil ourselves in God. To believe that we can achieve our true potential without him is to turn our back on the thing that can bring us greatest hope. The New Age emphasis on our ability to improve ourselves – realise our true potential on our own or by going through certain exercises or meditating in a particular way – is its most damaging aspect.

New Age salvation

The New Age promises that it will help us to realise our true human potential. But it has no idea of salvation. It cannot have for it has no idea of sin. The Bible from Genesis to Revelation sees men and women as alienated from God because of sin. Sin is normally thought of as specific wrong actions. But at its heart it is rebellion against God, the idea that we can go our own way. We do not like the idea of sin. That is why we find New Age thinking so attractive. It permits us to believe that we can do things in our own strength, that we are potentially good. The Bible on the other hand sees us as sinners who need God to do something for us.

Sin has a number of effects. We have already looked at Colossians 1:21 and seen that we are God's enemies. This is a long way from the New Age idea that we are all potentially gods. Why are we God's enemies? Because of our 'evil behaviour'. We shall look later at the type of behaviour that God expects from his people. But for the moment notice that our behaviour matters. New Age thinking is not consistent on morality. Many New Agers have very high moral standards but no idea of any absolute values. We are asked to behave in certain ways, 'to fit in with the harmony of the planet', or 'for the good of humanity'. There is nothing wrong with considering either of these important, but they are hardly enough on which to build one's whole moral code.

Our behaviour has made us God's enemies and unless some change happens we are not going to be in a position to build a relationship with him. Paul puts it even more strongly in a verse we have looked at before:

> When you were dead in your sins and in the
> uncircumcision of your sinful nature.
>
> *Colossians 2:13*

The thought that we might be totally unable to do anything to improve our lot is unthinkable to the New Ager. Human potential is everything. But Paul has a different picture. And it is one that most of us will identify with. We know how hard it is to do the things we want to do. Much of our life is marked by the struggle to be something that we are not. The world is full of unhappy people. In a strange way, if only they could grasp the truth about sin they would begin to find something of the solution.

Imagine the person who goes to the doctor to be told that he has a malignant growth. It can be cured. All it will take is some simple surgery. The cure rate is high, the prognosis good. But he will not believe that there is anything seriously wrong. 'Nothing that a few days rest won't put right!' And off he goes. This looks to us like the height of folly. And so, no doubt, it would be. But we behave in much the same way when it comes to spiritual matters. Only when we recognise the nature of the problem are we in a position to bring about a cure. And the New Age denies the existence of the problem.

When Paul issues his warning to the Colossians in 2:8, he has in mind something which owes its power to human reason and energy rather than to dependence on God.

> See to it that no-one takes you captive through
> hollow and deceptive philosophy, which depends on

> human tradition and the basic principles of this
> world rather than on Christ.   *Colossians 2:8*

This collection of human ideas is ultimately futile and
leaves people trapped. The New Age traps too. Those
who have started out with some innocent involvement
have found themselves drawn deeper and deeper into
something which they do not understand but find
strangely attractive. Several Christians who have
become involved with New Age groups have ultimately
lost their Christian faith.

It is strange that in a world like ours people continue to believe in the ability of humanity to resolve its
problems. As I write, civil war of the utmost barbarity
is taking place in Bosnia while the world looks on.
Vietnam, Cambodia, Sudan, Mozambique, Somalia,
Angola, Liberia – all have found themselves in similar
situations within the last twenty years. Repressive
regimes exist in many parts of the world and crush
opposition with ruthless brutality – who can forget
Tiananmen square? Freedom fighters (or terrorists, it
all depends on one's viewpoint) conduct their campaigns
with little thought for the consequences. And all this on
the heels of a war which engulfed most of the globe
and brought the unbelievable horrors of the Holocaust.

Who turned out the light?

Because New Age thinking, or for that matter, secular
humanism, has no place for sin, it has no place for
anything like the Christian understanding of salvation.
We shall take a closer look at what this actually is in
part two of this book. But for our present purpose we

need to note that the way in which God has dealt with human sin is in the person of Jesus Christ. Verses we have already looked at make this clear:

> ... giving thanks to the Father, who has qualified you to share in the inheritance of the saints in the kingdom of light. For he has rescued us from the dominion of darkness and brought us into the kingdom of the Son he loves, in whom we have redemption [through his blood], the forgiveness of sins.
> *Colossians 1:12–14*

This is miles from any idea of self-improvement. It is a picture of humanity in a mess – a mess it cannot get out of on its own. When he speaks of the dominion of darkness, Paul describes people who are held captive.

The tragedy is that they genuinely believe that they are free. A dog on a chain may think that it can run wherever it chooses, but its movement is limited by the length of the chain. To be under the dominion of darkness is to have the range of our choices limited – but to be unaware of it. The decisions which seem to be our own, which seem to be made freely, are actually determined by something else.

This is not to say that everyone is directly controlled by some evil force. It is not to say that those who do not believe in Jesus are incapable of doing good. But if we take the Bible seriously we have to say that they are not the free agents they think they are. Often we find ourselves doing things that we do not want to do. Often we find ourselves struggling to do the things that we want to do. This is being under the dominion of darkness.

Darkness is linked to the idea of deception. There is an illusion of freedom, there is a suggestion of hope, but it is founded on a lie. This has been the way of things since the Devil put out the first great lie in Eden. He offered hope but delivered disappointment.

When my son first went up a slide in a children's playground he was confident that he could manage without my help. He was, after all, a grown-up, sophisticated three-year-old; or he was at the foot of the steps. He was still a sophisticated three-year-old at the top of the steps. Until it came to having to step on to the slide and come down. At this point father had to come to the rescue, pushing past a queue of other children on the steps. My son had deceived himself because he could only see part of the picture. Being in the darkness is rather like this.

Against this, what God promises us is light. We 'share in the inheritance of the saints in the kingdom of light'. There seems to be something in the human make-up that longs for light. Interestingly, it is one of the themes of the New Age. Shirley McLaine, who is perhaps more responsible for the popularisation of New Age thinking in the USA than anyone else, entitled one of her books *Dancing in the Light*. Light was also a popular theme in the Gnostic thinking of the second century. It could well have been a part of the heretical teaching which was going the rounds in Colossae. If so, Paul takes up the language of his opponents to show that true light can be found only in Jesus. He alone meets the deepest longings of humanity.

The Christian response

How are we to respond to all of this? There are two opposite reactions. Some Christians, seeing the profound dangers of the New Age, behave as though anyone who ever has a massage or visits an osteopath is demon-possessed. The whole thing becomes a gigantic conspiracy and we have to be on our guard – for even the most innocent things can take on New Age associations. I was recently solemnly assured that the bead seat I have in my car is New Age!

At the other extreme are those who try to add New Age thinking to Christianity. St James' Church in London's Piccadilly has acquired something of a reputation as a New Age Church. And you can certainly find a whole range of things on offer, from shiatsu to Jungian psychology. A recent brochure for the Alternatives programme – which admittedly includes a disclaimer ('Although St James's Church, in its openness of mind includes Alternatives, the ideas in the Alternatives programme are not representative of St James's Church itself.') lists an approach to Tibetan meditation, a workshop on 'a specific technique of meditation and inner energy work to transform deep-rooted attitudinal patterns', and an introduction to the core ideas and methods of Shamanism.

This approach is exemplified in the following report:

> 'Where politics has failed to save the planet, religion is taking over. A Christian priest last night launched Britain's first festival of "green" spirituality . . . Robert Van de Weyer . . . the first speaker in a month-long festival that stretches from Newcastle

upon Tyne to Cornwall and encompasses beliefs as diverse as druidism, deep ecology and Islam. . . In Leicester next week, Faith in Nature, described as the most comprehensive multi-faith environmental project undertaken, will include worshippers from the Baha'i, Christian, Hare Krishna, Hindu, Jain, Jewish and Sikh communities. . . . Francis Miller, of the Centre for Creation Spirituality, says that unlike fundamentalism, which views Jesus as unique, green Christianity offers a view of divinity within nature which can be shared with other faiths.'

The Independent, 11 September, 1992

In working out how we are to respond we can learn from Paul. He was always open to the way in which evil powers could delude individuals. He had no time for diluting the message about Jesus with other ideas. But there is no hint in Paul of the paranoia which strikes at some Christians. Paul did not find the demonic behind every bush. Christians could happily eat food which had been offered to idols as long as they did not participate in idol worship (see 1 Corinthians 8:1–13; 10:14–22).

He would have us be discerning and would want us to be clear about what we believe. We do need to be on our guard, for New Age thinking crops up in many places and can have a look of innocence about it. My daughter encountered it in a music lecture in her first week at University. Others will meet it in business training courses. John Drane, in his book *What is the New Age saying to the Church?*, has a disturbing story of a man who lost his job and was offered psychiatric treatment by his former employers because his Christian principles were in conflict with the New Age content of the management course he had been sent on. A recent holiday programme on TV featured a health farm, once the preserve of healthy exercise and rabbit food. No more it would seem – along with massage comes meditation.

All this constitutes a challenge not unlike the one that Paul faced. The popularity of the New Age shows that people are longing for a sense of the spiritual. We can give it to them. But some of us need to rediscover it for ourselves; the church has failed, partly because it has become dry with little sense of wonder or of God. That is why, above all, Paul takes us back to Jesus as the centre of our faith. He emphasises that truth, salvation and victory are all found in Jesus. He wants us to witness to him, being sensitive to the convictions of others. And he wants us to place our own faith firmly in him in the midst of a confusing world. It was through doing this that Paul made his impact in the confusing world of the first century.

PART 2
CHRIST AND THE CHURCH

5

CALLED

OUT OF

DARKNESS

When I was ten my parents returned to Africa as missionaries. I could imagine what to expect – after all I'd been five when we'd left before. I'd seen pictures, read books, listened to others talk. But the reality! I can still remember vividly the two-day train journey from Beira to Blantyre – the heat, the smells, the brown earth, the dark nights pin-pricked with the light of fires, the life and activity of the stations – nothing had prepared me for how wonderful it all was.

The world had been waiting for Jesus but only faint outlines could be seen, like a shadow thrown on to the wall by a distant light. When he comes all is clear. It is as though, with his arrival, an otherwise dim room is flooded with light. Hence John's description at the start of his gospel: 'The true light that gives light to every man' (John 1:9), an idea that Jesus himself confirmed by talking of himself as the light of the world (John 8:12; 9:5). The mystery, as we saw in an earlier chapter, once hidden, is now revealed.

What is revealed is the significance not only of Jesus' birth and life but also of his death. The revelation takes place in the arrival of Jesus and *in his departure*. The mystery concerns salvation, and for Paul that can only mean the cross. We return to familiar verses:

> . . . and through him to reconcile to himself all things, whether things on earth or things in heaven, by making peace through his blood, shed on the cross. Once you were alienated from God and were enemies in your minds because of your evil behaviour. But now he has reconciled you by Christ's physical body through death to present you holy in his sight, without blemish and free from accusation.   *Colossians 1:20–22*

This was the heart of the gospel as Paul had understood it. We have already seen the extent of our alienation from God, and that the only way back is through the death of Jesus on the cross. But for modern men and women this doesn't make much sense. I remember talking with someone after an evening communion service – a lady who had been associated with the church for several years, and was an active and effective worker. She had begun to explore other ways of looking at things. She stood beside me and said with some anger in her voice, 'I just don't see what difference a man dying 2000 years ago can make to my life today. It doesn't make any sense.'

Who's in charge?

This lady's attitude is a common one – and an under-
standable one. It reflects the contemporary desire to live
without God. Society has become increasingly secular.
We've already met the phrase 'man come of age' which
became popular sometime during the sixties. To come
of age was to be no longer tied to the apron strings of
a nanny-god, who monitored every action and looked
down with faint disapproval, or beholden to a 'Father
Christmas' god who showered down his gifts with
gentle and well-meaning benevolence but robbed people
of their independence.

We have already commented on this desire for independence – the central problem from Adam and Eve
onwards – and seen that the results have not been spec-
tacularly impressive. Our twentieth century 'adult'
humanity must take responsibility for an unparalleled
set of horrors – including the Somme, Belsen, the Gulag
Archipelago, Beirut, the killing fields of Cambodia and
Sarajevo. A look at contemporary culture – the point-
lessness and futility of modernism, the strange nostalgia
and anarchy of post-modernism, suggests a lost rather
than a visionary race. If one also considers the aborted
foetuses, the battered wives, the abused children and
the young people begging in the heart of our most
sophisticatd Western cities, one wonders why men and
women should believe that they can make a better show
of running the world on their own.

This is not to say that we have always done better
when we have claimed to let God have control. Many
episodes in the history of the Church should fill us with
shame rather than with pride. But if we are honest

the shameful episodes have occurred when men (and it normally was *men*) have preferred to trust in their own wisdom than to listen to what God might want to say. Humanity, through the ages, does not have a good record of managing on its own. As obvious as this may seem it is not a lesson we find easy to learn! We still like to believe that we are in control.

The idea of the cross cuts across all of this. For Paul the cross was good news because it offered hope to people who had no way of making it on their own. In earlier chapters we looked at the problems created by sin, but as a diagnosis of the human condition 'we are sinful' has little support. The very word, 'sin' sounds old fashioned. We prefer to think of ourselves as essentially good. The fact that this flies in the face of the evidence doesn't seem to bother us. We would prefer to think that we have been inflicted with a temporary madness, that we are sick, that we are living in the wrong environment. Any explanation will do as long as it does not involve the admission that we are, at heart, plain bad.

But plain bad is what the Bible says that we are. No explanation of the behaviour that leads to Belsen, Beirut or Bosnia makes sense until we understand this. The darkness of our age, or of any other, originates in the evil which lies in the heart of men and women. Whatever else the story of Genesis 1–3 teaches us it is that God made us to enjoy a relationship with him. Sin caused our alienation from God and gave rise to a settled attitude of rebellion against him. The church has failed modern society by going along with the thinking that sin can be conveniently argued away. There is little place for the ranting preacher of so much caricature;

shouting at people that they are all sinners does not get us very far. But we can offer a thoughtful analysis of modern society and its ills which brings sin back into the picture.

We would feel cheated if we went to the doctor, and before asking us the problem or making an examination, he wrote out a prescription and sent us off to take three tablets a day. We would wonder what condition he was treating. We would be even more worried if the surgeon wheeled us straight into the theatre without making an examination.

Without an analysis of the problem we cannot provide the answer. Modern people may not want to hear about sin – just as they may not want to be told that they have cancer. But unless they are told, there is no hope of a cure. As Christians we need to bring sin and evil back into people's vocabulary – not in the self-righteous, 'holier than thou' manner of the 'repent for the end is nigh' sandwich-board man, but in the manner of fellow sufferers who have found a cure.

The diagnosis is only the beginning. As I discovered on a recent visit to the doctor, there is something rather depressing about having a problem described (in my case painful but not life-threatening) and then to be told that nothing can be done for it. What we really want is a cure. For sin the cure is the cross. But it seems that the church has lost confidence in the cross. It disturbs us, because we cannot fully explain why God should choose to act in such a way, and some Christian theologians have told us that the idea of God dying for us is morally unacceptable.

Friends again

Paul has many rich pictures to explain the effect of the cross on our lives. In these verses the emphasis is on bringing peace to those who are at war, and friendship to those who are alienated. In modern Western society alienation is one of the great problems. Individuals feel very much alone. In our cities many move from an isolated bedsit to a job in which they feel undervalued back to the loneliness of the bedsit. For many the thought of a bedsit would be a luxury – their only home is a cardboard box.

Alex Haley's *Roots*, both the book and subsequent TV programme, achieved popularity because he touched on this nerve of alienation, on our need to belong. There lies a longing in most of us for something beyond. It is almost as if, buried deep within the human consciousness, there is a memory of a place we left long ago, somewhere we would feel really at home, but cannot reach.

The cross changes this, because it is the way in which God brings us peace. And in bringing us peace, God gives us the feeling that we have come home, that we are now where we ought to be. Once we were fighting against all that was best for us but now we can relax, secure in the knowledge that we have arrived. The child that constantly fights with her parents will never find security, but once she relaxes in the parental arms she finds warmth and love.

The biblical idea of peace is a full and rich one. For us the word normally means little more than the absence of conflict, but the Hebrew word for peace, shalom, conjures up a picture of well-being, of prosperity, of wholeness, of being at one with everything. It comes from a root that means to make whole or to make complete. And that is what God has done. Like a vase that has lain shattered in pieces on the floor and been patiently put back together again, an object of beauty and usefulness, so he deals with us. Right now our cracks can still be seen, but one day even they will become invisible.

To be at war with God has other effects. It means, for example, that we are not at peace with ourselves. To attack God is to attack ourselves. Many people are obviously self-destructive – addictive behaviour is one of the great curses of the modern world. We see it at its most obvious in lives that are destroyed by drug or alcohol abuse. But at a different level there are those who are addicted to sex, to eating or to shopping. Such people are neither whole nor free. They are broken and trapped. When Jesus makes peace through the cross it is to deal with broken lives like these.

To be at war with God is to see the whole of creation thrown out of joint. The rebellion of Adam and Eve resulted in chaos throughout nature. Hence the disasters, the toil, the sense of alienation from the world. But the peace that Jesus brings aims not simply at individual well-being but at a whole new creation, free from the problems and strains of the one we know. This is why Paul can talk of God reconciling all things. Too often we have seen the Christian hope as something for individuals. It is far more wonderful than that. It is for the whole universe (see Romans 8:17–21).

Rescue service

Talk of freedom naturally leads on to a second picture which Paul uses to help us understand what the cross achieves:

> ... giving thanks to the Father, who has qualified you to share in the inheritance of the saints in the kingdom of light. For he has rescued us from the dominion of darkness and brought us into the kingdom of the Son he loves, in whom we have redemption [through his blood], the forgiveness of sins.   *Colossians 1:12–14*

Again we come back to what is becoming a familiar passage – and so it should for these are key verses. We have seen before the extent of the control which evil has over us. Here Paul uses the word dominion. Elsewhere he describes us as slaves of sin. A slave is under the dominion of his master. He has no freedom of his own. He cannot decide what he will do today or where he will go – his every action is limited by his master's will.

The powers that we looked at in chapter 2 have control over our lives. They give rise to the destructive patterns of behaviour that we looked at in the last section. One of the great ironies of modern life is that women and men like to think that they are at last free, but this sense of freedom is an illusion.

When Iraq invaded Kuwait, the Kuwaits came under the domination of a greater power. Only by putting together an international force and sending it in to drive out the Iraqi armies could their freedom be restored. Consider what God has done for us. Through

Christ he has driven back the powers that held us, and set us free.

Free to do our own thing, to run our own lives as we choose? Well, not exactly! God has rescued us from the dominion of darkness and brought us into the kingdom of the Son he loves. There is a contrast between being under dominion and belonging to a kingdom. The first sounds heavy and oppressive, the second carries with it the idea of acceptance, of security, of something that we are happy to be part of. So while there are obligations and responsibilities they are not imposed like those of the dominion of darkness, and while there are duties we are not driven to them forcibly.

At the start of his ministry Jesus is revealed as God's beloved son (Matthew 3:17). John, in the opening verses of his gospel, speaks of Jesus as God's only Son (John 1:18). God the Father and God the Son work together to rescue sinful people. The plan to rescue us was devised in the eternal and loving heart of the triune God. We are now, therefore, members of a kingdom founded on love. Once we were under the dominion of powers whose whole existence is based on hatred.

The rescue is complete. The cold, weak canoeists have been brought safely to land, given warm blankets, nourishing food, and restored to the arms of those they love. We have left fear and hopelessness behind: we are now in a place of security and peace.

Getting the qualifications

We were under the dominion of darkness, but we have come into the kingdom of light. It is hard for those of us who live in the cities of the West to understand exactly what this means. I am writing this on holiday in a small cabin in a forest in the Quantocks. Currently suffering with sciatica I find that a twenty-minute brisk walk before I go to bed helps me sleep. At home this is no problem – there are street lights everywhere. On the first night here there was thick cloud cover and no moon. My torch could only illuminate a small part of the path ahead. Everything else was totally black. Although I know the area well I found it difficult to locate the gate back into the site where the cabin stands. I was reminded of my teenage years in Africa when we lived on a mission station, a quarter of a mile from the nearest house with no street lighting and no electricity. Except on moonlit nights some form of light was essential to avoid losing the path, tripping over a fallen branch or awkward rock or stepping on a sleeping snake.

Paul has similar pictures in his mind. Darkness leads to isolation, fear and uncertainty. Light brings clarity and certainty. The kingdom of darkness is no place to be. The kingdom of light is much more appealing. But how do we get there? What must we do? The answer is clear – nothing! We already have the necessary qualifications.

The job advert sounded so attractive. They wanted a degree in French and mine was in Theology but maybe it wouldn't matter. It did, of course. Without the right qualifications there is little chance of getting a particular job. A friend of mine once received an invitation to a Buckingham Palace garden party. Had I simply walked up to the gate of the Palace I would not have been allowed in, but he had only to appear with the invitation in his hand to have the gate opened. He had the right qualifications, I hadn't.

So when it comes to entering the kingdom of light, the kingdom of God's Son, we don't have to worry about our lack of qualifications – all the qualifications we need are waiting for us at the door. Our entry is guaranteed, not on the basis of our performance but on the performance of Jesus.

The price is paid

Paul has problems getting across the full wonder of what this is all about. We are rescued, we are qualified, we are bought. These are the ideas behind the term redemption. The picture in Paul's mind would have been of the market place, and perhaps especially of the slave market, for the Greek word had become an almost technical term for the purchase of freedom for a slave.

This is how his Gentile readers would have understood the term. But some of the sizeable Jewish population in Colossae had become Christians. They would have seen another meaning in Paul's word – a meaning which would inevitably have been in the mind of Paul the Jew. Their minds would have gone back to the Exodus when all the Egyptian firstborn died while the Hebrew firstborn were spared. From that point on all the firstborn animals, and sons, belonged to God but could be redeemed by the payment of a price (see Exodus 13:13–16). The Exodus itself, the deliverance from Egypt, is frequently described in the Old Testament as an act of redemption.

Again the idea of freedom emerges. Rescue implies being saved from some situation of distress. Redemption implies being freed from captivity or bondage. The price has been paid.

Even this does not exhaust the ideas included in redemption; there is also the idea of ownership. Israel was freed from the slavery of Egypt to enter the service of God. To enter into God's service is not to exchange one bondage for another; it is to enter the service of one 'whose service is perfect freedom'. Or to use the words of the old hymn,

> Make me a captive, Lord,
> And then I shall be free. . .

One of the ways in which we experience freedom is through forgiveness. Guilt can trap us in ways that few other things can. If we have offended or damaged another there can be no relief until we have sorted it out and know that we are forgiven. This is just as important in our relationship with God. That is why Paul talks here about redemption and forgiveness in the same breath. Only when we know that we are forgiven will we know true freedom. Sometimes, however, we find it hard to believe that God has forgiven us, and even harder to forgive ourselves. At such times we need to understand that it was in order to obtain forgiveness that Christ died, and hold on to that.

Truth and hope

We have spoken of danger, of darkness, of captivity: these are the problems which beset people in any age, and our age is no exception. The world is still a danger-ous place. Dangerous as a result of increasing levels of violence at both the personal and the national level.

Dangerous because of economic recession and the consequent loss of livelihood. Dangerous because of the uncertain future of the planet in the light of our appalling record of squandering its limited resources.

The world is a dark place. Nameless fears cripple many people. Ignorance and selfishness lead to oppressive and ruthless exploitation of the weak. The old and the young in many societies are at risk. Moral standards have been cut loose from the absolute values which previous generations knew, and people do as they choose.

Our captivity is shown in many ways. The economic system under which we live reduces our options – and it makes little difference whether the system is socialist or capitalist. The constant desire for more so that we may retain our place in the social order drives us to decisions we might not otherwise make. Most of us, to some degree or another, have our choices limited by behavioural habits we cannot change or by fault lines in our personalities created, perhaps, by past hurts. No one is truly free.

So a message which addresses these issues comes as a great relief:

> . . . because we have heard of your faith in Christ Jesus and of the love you have for all the saints – the faith and love that spring from the hope that is stored up for you in heaven and that you have already heard about in the word of truth, the gospel that has come to you.   *Colossians 1:4–6*

The news came to the Colossians as truth and as gospel. Truth is in short supply. Our leaders rarely tell us the truth. Tonight's news has been taken up with proposed pit closures in the UK – politicians backtracking, apologising, dealing in half the story – and the presidential election in the US, with George Bush and Bill Clinton making political capital by each misrepresenting the views of the other. We are given promises that cannot be kept – remember the famous, 'Watch my lips – no more taxes'?

Our religious leaders often seem no better. The scandals of some tele-evangelists leave the whole church tarnished. Other religions and the cults have the same problems. But in the gospel we have truth – something we can cling to in a world where everything else seems shifting and doubtful.

The Greek word for gospel, *euangelion*, simply means an announcement of something good. So this message of the cross of Jesus, delivered against the background of the problems of humanity, comes as truth and as good news. And it comes as good news to people who are constantly confronted by bad news.

Part of the good news is that what God offers, he offers freely. We are accustomed to the fact that nothing is for free. There are, as the saying goes, 'No free lunches'. If I give you a present at Christmas you will feel guilty if you do not give me one in return. The free offers of some timeshare salespeople have strings attached which have left many people ruined. But God offers us a new relationship with himself at no cost to us. All he looks for is 'faith in Christ Jesus'. Faith is often misunderstood. Evangelical Christians who have, since the Reformation, made much of faith over and against the idea of salvation by works, have sometimes made faith into a work, something which we have to do in order to earn our salvation. But faith is simply our response to what God has done. It is receiving. It is accepting that what God has done is sufficient. It is trusting that what he has done will work, and then being prepared to base our lives on this belief.

Faith recognises our own inability to do anything. This means that although we do not have to do anything, receiving God's offer is not particularly easy. Faith involves an admission of inadequacy, and that comes hard to many of us. Perhaps this is why the gospel comes as good news to the poor. They know their inadequacy. It is paraded before them every day. The rich, on the other hand, find it hard to enter the kingdom of heaven (Matthew 19:23), because they are used to feeling competent, to assuming that money will open doors, to having power and using it. The cross challenges the rich and powerful because it removes their power. It gives hope to the poor and powerless because it offers them a way that does not depend on possessing power.

Hope is a key word. Paul makes the point that our faith and our love spring from hope. There is not much hope in our world. Few people feel that they have much to look forward to. Life is a grind. Like the writer of the famous poem of Ecclesiastes we seem to go round in an endless, pointless circle. Two young undergraduates at Oxford, with apparently everything before them, have recently committed suicide, presumably because the future looked bleak to them rather than bright with hope. What the cross does is to transform our view of the future, so we have something to look forward to, someting to live for.

We need to be careful though. Christians have been accused, with some justification, of concentrating on the future at the expense of the present. We live in the here and now and it is in the here and now that the impact of the cross must be felt. It should be felt in at least three areas – our relationship with God, our relationship with other Christians and our relationship with the world.

It is natural that we should respond to God's redeeming love with gratitude and worship. However, if our worship stops at the singing of songs and the uttering of prayers in the safe walls of our churches or the security of our housegroups, we have not understood what it's all about. Christ's death is a death for the world beyond the church. It is good news for the hopeless. Amy Carmichael has a frightening vision of blind people walking hand in hand towards the edge of a cliff while others sit by and make daisy chains. The Church's current preoccupation with worship is a worthy reflection of God and what he has done but it can become an escape from our responsibilities, an 'inward lookingness' that denies the true purpose of the cross. True worship as the Bible describes it reaches out beyond the confines of God's people. It is for the world.

Having experienced God's salvation we can feel that we have arrived – we are chosen people, we are safe – and look at those 'outside' with a mixture of judgmentalism and pity. We fail to see that the life of Jesus was a life lived out in the world. This is the whole point of the gospel story – the Word became flesh and lived among us, not apart from us. The cross stands at the interface of the kingdom of God and the kingdom of this world and makes its mark on both. It is not for us Christians alone – it is for all humanity. It is not the private property of the Christian, it is the public proclamation of God's love for the world.

This leads to an important point that we touched on before but do not have time to look at in depth. Christ's death is not simply for individual salvation; it is for the redemption of the whole universe. Through his death he overturns all the evil that came in with human rebellion. We can look forward to a new heaven and a new earth. This is the heart of the Christian hope.

We confront the darkness of the world with the light which shines from the cross of Jesus Christ. We shall not do this while the cross remains hidden among us. We take it out joyfully into the market places of the world. Michael Green captures it beautifully on the *Person to Person* video:

> 'If you look in the Acts of the Apostles the people that spread the gospel were the nameless little men ... they were just chattering. They couldn't keep quiet in the wine shops, in the laundries, on the street corners of the ancient world. These were the places you met people. And if you and I did that a bit more in the pub, in the parent's association, at school, at work – just to say a word of commendation of Jesus we would find that the Holy Spirit picks up some of these things and people say, 'Hey, tell me more; I'd like to know.'

6

CHANGING
FROM
DARKNESS

'Life was so miserable; I was isolated and lonely. Then twelve years ago I asked Jesus into my life and it was wonderful. He could change your life too.' End of story. We've all heard things like this. But there's a problem; they give the impression that being a follower of Jesus is simply about some event in the past.

It is one thing to rejoice in the knowledge that we have been rescued from the danger, qualified to enter the kingdom, and brought back into freedom. It is another to sit back and congratulate ourselves. The Christian life cannot be confined to a one-off conversion experience in the past; it must be expressed in a continuing commitment. Many things can divert us. Paul encourages the Colossians to press on, even when other things look more attractive.

I want you to know how much I am struggling for you and for those at Laodicea, and for all who have not met me personally. My purpose is that they may be encouraged in heart and united in love, so that they may have the full riches of complete understanding, in order that they may know the mystery of God, namely, Christ, in whom are hidden all the treasures of wisdom and knowledge. I tell you this so that no-one may deceive you by fine-sounding arguments. For though I am absent from you in body, I am present with you in spirit and delight to see how orderly you are and how firm your faith in Christ is. So then, just as you received Christ Jesus as Lord, continue to live in him, rooted and built up in him, strengthened in the faith as you were taught, and overflowing with thankfulness. See to it that no-one takes you captive through hollow and deceptive philosophy, which depends on human tradition and the basic principles of this world rather than on Christ. For in Christ all the fulness of the Deity lives in bodily form, and you have been given fulness in Christ, who is the Head over every power and authority. In him you were also circumcised in the putting off of the sinful nature, not with a circumcision done by the hands of men but with the circumcision done by Christ, having been buried with him in baptism and raised with him through your faith in the power of God, who raised him from the dead. When you were dead in your sins and in the uncircumcision of your sinful nature, God made you alive with Christ. He forgave us all our sins, having cancelled the written code, with its regulations, that was against us and that stood opposed to us; he took it away, nailing it to the cross. And having disarmed the powers and authorities, he made a public spectacle of them, triumphing over them by the cross.

Therefore do not let anyone judge you by what you eat or drink, or with regard to a religious festival, a New Moon celebration or a Sabbath day. These are a shadow of the things that were to come; the reality, however, is found in Christ. Do not let anyone who delights in false humility and the worship of angels disqualify you for the prize. Such a person goes into great detail about what he has seen, and his unspiritual mind puffs him up with idle notions. He has lost connection with the Head, from whom the whole body, supported and held together by its ligaments and sinews, grows as God causes it to grow. Since you died with Christ to the basic principles of this world, why, as though you still belonged to it, do you submit to its rules: 'Do not handle! Do not taste! Do not touch!'? These are all destined to perish with use, because they are based on human commands and teachings. Such regulations indeed have an appearance of wisdom, with their self-imposed worship, their false humility and their harsh treatment of the body, but they lack any value in restraining sensual indulgence.

Colossians 2:1–23

The goal

A small baby left to itself will not survive for long. Nor for that matter will an adult left in freezing temperatures without adequate protection. Put any of us into a hostile environment and we are in danger. And, make no mistake, Christians are in a hostile environment. If we are to make an impact on our world rather than be weakened by it, we need to grow up and to develop strength and resolve.

God's goal is to make us mature. When a baby does not develop properly there is something wrong, and the same is true when Christians fail to mature. But growing up can be a painful business. It involves letting some of our early securities go; it involves stepping out into areas we would rather avoid; it involves facing challenges to our faith head on.

This is why Paul is so concerned. He knows there are plenty of alternative philosophies setting out their stalls in Colossae, claiming special revelations from God, and offering more pleasurable lifestyles and more acceptable beliefs. It was attractive to people then to go along with these ideas, to be part of the in-crowd. It is equally attractive to us now when we face similar challenges. To resist we need to be mature – to know what we believe, to have a firm attachment to it and the courage to stand for it. But how do we become mature?

God told me

The idea of a hot-line to God appeals to many. Most of the cults whose members invade our doorsteps or accost us in the streets started out with a claim to some new revelation from God. This pattern of adding to the Bible is repeated time and time again in history. Christians are not immune. The attraction of having a hot-line to God, and using it to get power over others, has proved too great a temptation for some. In the early days of charismatic renewal many were deeply hurt because they gained the impression that they were second-class citizens. Those who have some special experience can very easily suggest, without intending to, that they are therefore more holy, closer to God, have more knowledge and more right to determine the direction of the church. Sometimes, and this is much worse, they suggest these things deliberately. There are too many horror stories of people whose lives have been damaged by misdirected prophecies for us to be complacent. A few days before writing this section I was talking with someone who was being told by the elders of her church that she was outside God's will because she would not move house.

Paul had met people who misused this sort of power. He describes them in this passage. They go into great detail about what they have seen. Then, because they are unspiritual, they become arrogant. But their ideas are of no real value. Exactly what was gong on in Colossae isn't easy to say. But we can be fairly certain that someone was claiming special authority on the basis of a vision. In Paul's view their humility and spirituality were false. In their eagerness to hear God they had overstepped the mark. In the end they were really more concerned to have their own way; in the end they did not present God's message but empty ideas of their own.

Special revelations have their place. Paul himself experienced them. He met with Jesus in a somewhat unusual way on the road to Damascus (Acts 9:1–9). It is generally thought that when he describes a man being caught up into the third heaven (2 Corinthians 12:1–4) he is talking about himself. However, when Paul experiences special revelations he always does two things. First, he checks out what God is saying against his understanding of Scripture, and second, he checks it out with other respected Christian leaders – and not only those who might be expected to agree with him!

We have his own description of how he went about this in Galatians 1:10–24. The gospel he preached came straight from God by revelation. But he still went up to Jerusalem to spend time with Peter; if he had it wrong Peter could have put him right. Paul also made sure that he checked out everything against the Old Testament, the only Bible he had. Useful lessons here for us!

Visions and words from God are good; they show that God is alive and that he is in touch with us. But those who have them are not automatically better Christians, or holier Christians or even more effective Christians. A word from God doesn't give us all the answers and it certainly doesn't give us the right to tell others what they should be doing.

It's all in the way I live

We like things to be clear-cut. When we go to the doctor we'd much rather hear her say, 'Take these tablets for a week and you will be fine' than be told no one is entirely sure what is wrong or what treatment might help.

Because we like things to be straightforward we try to reduce everything to a set of rules and regulations. If we do this and don't do that, then God will accept us. If we just keep the rules we will become mature Christians. Churches are full of people who know how it should be done. They are quick to condemn those who don't match up to their standards. They had their counterparts in the church in Colossae. Paul warns against them:

> Since you died with Christ to the basic principles of
> this world, why, as though you still belonged to it,
> do you submit to its rules: 'Do not handle! Do not
> taste! Do not touch!'? These are all destined to
> perish with use, because they are based on human
> commands and teachings. Such regulations indeed
> have an appearance of wisdom, with their self-
> imposed worship, their false humility and their
> harsh treatment of the body, but they lack any value
> in restraining sensual indulgence.
>
> *Colossians 2:20–23*

Sounds impressive, looks good, creates the right
appearances. For some of the Colossians the important
things were steering clear of certain foods, avoiding
certain actions. They were only concerned with what
showed on the surface. Some years ago I went to buy a
car. While the salesman was telling me how good the car
was and how it had just been resprayed, I was lying
underneath it pulling off large lumps of rusty
metal. The respray had made it look good but had not
changed the really important things. Religion based
only on external behaviour is equally dangerous.
Forms of Christianity which tell us that the way to
become more mature is to keep all the rules are no
exception.

Like some of the Colossians, the Galatians had
opted for a religion based on keeping rules. Paul had
some hard words for them:

> You foolish Galatians! Who has bewitched you?
> Before your very eyes Jesus Christ was clearly
> portrayed as crucified. I would like to learn just one

thing from you: Did you receive the Spirit by
observing the law, or by believing what you heard?
Galatians 5:1, 2

To have seen that we are put right with God by trusting
in what he has done for us and then to go back to
trying to win his approval by observing a complex set
of rules and regulations is like being released from
prison only to head straight back again. But this is
what we so often do. People are thought to be mature
Christians when they dress in certain ways, avoid specific things, adopt particular patterns of behaviour. Each
group will have his own set of rules. Among English
evangelical Christians in the fifties and sixties drinking
alcohol was definitely out – a mark of worldliness and
lukewarm devotion to Christ. An English Christian was
being entertained by evangelical friends in Germany,
and was offered a beer with his meal. When he
explained that this was considered unacceptable in
England, his host proceeded to give thanks for the meal,
including a prayer that his English brother might be
delivered from such a negative attitude to God's good
gifts. The issue is a complex one, but the incident demonstrates that the rules we make are often governed not
by the gospel but by cultural considerations. If we see
things on the basis of rules either the Englishman or the
German had it wrong, but both believed they were right.

If we are not careful, rules become negative. They
leave us feeling that we have failed unless, of course,
we keep them all, in which case we become self-righteous and forget that we are saved by what God has
done, not by what we have done ourselves. Rules make
us judgmental; they encourage us to look down on those

who have not moved as far along the path of holiness as we have. Rules enable us to create boundaries which exclude those with whom we feel uncomfortable. All of these attitudes are unholy rather than holy.

The best rule-keepers in the history of God's people were the Pharisees. They knew them all and kept rigourous checklists to demonstrate how well they were doing. But Jesus was not impressed with their maturity or holiness.

> Woe to you, teachers of the law and Pharisees, you hypocrites! You give a tenth of your spices – mint, dill and cummin. But you have neglected the more important matters of the law – justice, mercy and faithfulness. You should have practised the latter, without neglecting the former. You blind guides! You strain a gnat but swallow a camel.
>
> *Matthew 23:23–24*

Keeping a list of rules does not, then, seem to be the way to maturity.

Great time of worship

One of the great benefits of the renewal that the Church has experienced in the last thirty years has been the introduction of new patterns of worship that are joyous, spontaneous and which, at their best, reflect the character of God and the inspiration of his Spirit. Worship honours God. It can draw us closer to him and have a profound effect on our spiritual growth. But even at its best it is not, in and of itself, the key to growth or to maturity. We assume that if we have had a good time that we have met with God. In fact we may only have done things that bring us satisfaction. Our endless songs may have left no space for God and, for all our much vaunted prophecies, the voice of God may not have been heard. We feel good but we have not been changed. In fact being changed may sometimes mean that we feel bad – not a popular idea in our self-indulgent world.

So when Paul warns the Colossian Christians about the emptiness of these things we need to take notice:

> Do not let anyone who delights in false humility and the worship of angels disqualify you for the prize.
>
> *Colossians 2:18*

Now, worshipping angels may not be a great problem in your church. For Colossae it was a literal problem, because of the way people thought in the first century. The basic principle for them and for us is the same, however. Here were people who believed that their worship made them superior. In our own time, even sincere worship can bring problems. Whenever it becomes an end in itself, something we see in isolation, we are in danger of moving away from God rather than towards him. Worship can become an idol.

Keep close

So, if visions and words from God, keeping the rules and giving time to worship do not ensure growth in the Christian life, what does?

> So then, just as you received Christ Jesus as Lord, continue to live in him, rooted and built up in him,

> strengthened in the faith as you were taught, and
> overflowing with thankfulness.   *Colossians 2:6, 7*

Here is the key. Christian maturity and Christian holiness come through staying close to Jesus. They are relational not 'regulational'. They flow from true heart commitment not from outward activity.

Our goal in becoming mature is to become like Jesus (Romans 8:29). Often we become concerned about God's will for our lives. *This* is his will – for us to become like Jesus. We have something worth aiming for. But we shall only become like Jesus if we get to know him well and spend time in his company. The twelve disciples spent three years with Jesus. They walked with him, talked with him, ate with him and drank with him. They saw him first thing in the morning and they saw him last thing at night. They saw him under pressure and they saw him at parties. They heard his teaching and they saw his miracles. This was their apprenticeship.

Much as we might like to, we can't spend three years wandering about Palestine with Jesus. But we can determine to spend as much time with him as we can. Time with him in the Bible – not just a quick reading of our favourite verses but slow, lingering reading, reading as we might a letter from our husband, wife, girlfriend or boyfriend. Reading not to gain facts but to meet with the One we love.

And time with him in prayer. Not only, not even primarily, prayer that comes and asks him to do things for us, but prayer that enjoys his company, prayer that talks about the things of every day, prayer that listens. Once we have learnt to pray in this way, to be quiet and allow the Spirit to direct us, we shall draw close to

Jesus, and we shall find that our attitudes and our behaviour are shaped by what we discover of him and by what he does in our lives.

Time with him too, in the company of others. Meeting together is important (Hebrews 10:25). It gives us the opportunity to support and encourage one another. The example of others enjoying the presence of God stimulates us to know him better and gives us something to aim at. We can help one another to find God in new ways as we talk about our different experiences of him. We can pray for one another when the going is tough.

In all of this it is worth remembering that it can be helpful to make special times and places. For some people a routine and a disciplined approach provides the best framework. But we can also develop the habit of using the odd moments of the day for thinking of God and talking with him, wherever we are and whatever we are doing. We can learn a lot from Brother Lawrence, the lay brother in a French Carmelite monastery in the seventeenth century who discovered the secret of meeting with God among the washing up:

> 'The time of business,' said he, 'does not differ from the time of prayer; and in the noise and clutter of my kichen, while at the same time several persons are calling for different things, I can possess God in as great a tranquility as if I were upon my knees at the Blessed Sacrament.'

In touch with the Head

For Paul relationship with Jesus is essential, because our spiritual life flows from him:

> He has lost connection with the Head, from whom
> the whole body, supported and held together by its
> ligaments and sinews, grows as God causes it to grow.
>
> *Colossians 2:19*

A body without a head cannot grow. All the normal pro cesses are controlled by the brain and without it we are dead. But here Paul pictures a Christian who has lost touch with Jesus. For that person there can be no growth. All that makes for growth comes from him. Without him everything becomes uncontrolled and uncoordinated.

If we go back to verse 7 we see that we are to go on with Jesus in the same way that we received him. How did we receive him? By faith – faith in a crucified Saviour and a Living Lord. The cross isn't only the start of the Christian life, it is an essential element in our day-to-day progress. Each day, we come to the cross because there we recognise who we are and discover again the goodness and the love of God. Each day as we renew our commitment to God in the light of the cross, we acknowledge that we depend on him to carry on that work which he has started in our lives. Without this we become independent and attempt to do things on our own. The cross reminds us of our weakness and our sinfulness but at the same time offers us hope of change as we respond to the love of God.

We have received Jesus as Lord. We are, therefore, no longer free to determine exactly what we shall or shall not do. We are under obligation to do as Jesus asks. Growth involves realising our true God-given potential. Jesus shows what is possible and offers to lead us forward. We need to recognise that there will be obligations and responsibilities on our part. There can be no growth without obedience, and obedience is what having Jesus as Lord involves.

Paul uses two pictures to help us understand the nature of the relationship. We are to be rooted in Christ and we are to have our foundations in him. In October 1987 the South of England was rocked by the most violent storm for many years. By the time the wind finally died down many trees had been blown over exposing the full extent of the roots. It's suprising to discover just how far some roots go – if you've ever tried digging up an old rose bush you'll know all about it. Roots go down to the place where nutrients can be found and suck them up, enabling plants to grow. Tree roots provide stability in all but the fiercest of winds. They can penetrate even the most unlikely places – think of some of those trees you've seen growing on rocks with roots that have somehow found their way down through cracks to the place where there is good earth. We put our roots down into Jesus in the same sort of way, stopping at nothing until we have found the nourishment that he offers us.

The picture of foundations is similar. Look at the start of any large building and the first thing that impresses you is the depth of the foundations. A few years ago they built a new office opposite where I work. First they dug down, then they drilled deep holes and put in concrete piles. Without this the new building would soon have collapsed. Some friends of ours had just this problem with their house. Cracks appeared in the walls and they discovered that they actually had no foundations. The house had to be expensively underpinned. Mature people are stable people. And they are stable because they have foundations in Jesus.

Loaded with fruit

In our garden it has been a good year for blackcurrants. Nearly all the bushes are heavy with fruit. Another bumper crop. But there's one miserable bush on the end of the row that's thin and straggly, with only the odd blackcurrant here and there – for the second year running. This is the end of the road for that bush. In the autumn it will come out and be replaced by a new one.

> For this reason, since the day we heard about you, we have not stopped praying for you and asking God to fill you with the knowledge of his will through all spiritual wisdom and understanding. And we pray this in order that you may live a life worthy of the Lord and may please him in every way: bearing fruit in every good work, growing in the knowledge of God, being strengthened with all power according to his glorious might so that you may have great endurance and patience, and joyfully giving thanks to the Father, who has qualified you to share in the inheritance of the saints in the kingdom of light.   *Colossians 1:9–12*

A fruit tree that does not bear fruit is of little use to anyone. Christians, like fruit trees, are intended to bear fruit – the fruit of lives that demonstrate something of God's power and glory. Indeed this is the whole object of growing. So that we can point beyond ourselves to the One who has done this in us.

If you are anything like me you feel that the process of growing and changing is too slow. There are too many imperfections still in my life, too many things that I am ashamed of, too many attitudes that are unworthy of someone who has followed Jesus for years, too many actions that damage others. I become depressed and screw myself up to further action – only to find that I fail again. At such times I need to hear that change depends not on what I do but on what God through his great power is doing in me.

Paul quite deliberately piles three words on top of one another. We are being *strengthened*, with all God's *power*, according to his glorious *might*. The first two are the verb and the noun from the same root. In literal English we might say empowered with all power, but that would sound silly. In Greek the effect is of putting great emphasis on the statement. Paul does not want us to be in any doubt about the power that is available to us. The Greek word, incidentally, is the word which lies behind the English words dynamic and dynamite. When you wonder whether any change can come in your life, Colossians 1:9–12 is the place to look for reassurance.

> But now he has reconciled you by Christ's physical body through death to present you holy in his sight, without blemish and free from accusation – if you continue in your faith, established and firm, not moved from the hope held out in the gospel. This is the gospel that you heard and that has been proclaimed to every creature under heaven, and of which I, Paul, have become a servant. Now I rejoice in what was suffered for you, and I fill up in my flesh what is still lacking in regard to Christ's afflictions, for the sake of his body, which is the church. I have become its

> servant by the commission God gave me to present to
> you the word of God in its fulness – the mystery that
> has been kept hidden for ages and generations, but is
> now disclosed to the saints. To them God has chosen
> to make known among the Gentiles the glorious
> riches of this mystery, which is Christ in you, the
> hope of glory. We proclaim him, admonishing and
> teaching everyone with all wisdom, so that we may
> present everyone perfect in Christ. To this end I
> labour, struggling with all his energy, which so
> powerfully works in me.   *Colossians 1:22–29*

This is another reminder that God has done all that we need in Christ, that it is done through his cross. But notice how Paul puts it. It is through his 'physical body'. Jesus knows what it is like to struggle with all the pressures and temptations that we face. This is why the physical body is so important. There is a real earthy humanity about Jesus. This is not God playing at being human. Jesus knew hunger (Matthew 4:2), tiredness (John 4:6), fear (Matthew 26:40) and frustration (Matthew 26:40). He struggled as he faced the power of evil and when we go through the same struggle we know that he is no stranger to it.

Jesus shares our humanity so that we might share his character, through which we become (Romans 8:29). This process of change goes on throughout our lives, bringing us maturity. It does not come easily. There may well be pain and struggle, both as we long for our own maturity and for that of others.

Paul was so concerned for the growth of the Colossians that he went to great lengths. Obviously his suffering wasn't the same as that of Jesus. He couldn't die to save the Colossians – or anyone else for that matter. But as he went through the physical pain of travelling around the world preaching, being beaten and stoned for his troubles, he knew something of what Jesus felt. As he went through the emotional pain of sitting alongside some struggling Christian, or seeing someone who had started well falling away, he experienced something of the pain that Jesus feels.

When we were younger, my father received word in the middle of a family holiday that one of the young people in the church of which he was pastor was in spiritual difficulties. After a brief family conference he caught the next train home. None of us thought it strange. We shared his concern and we shared his pain. Many others reading this will have responded in similar ways.

Like Paul and like his Master before him, we respond to need out of love for others. One of the causes of the darkness in our world is its lack of love. So many lonely, isolated people, so many going home night after night to an empty house, so many with no house to go home to. What the world needs in the face of this darkness is the love which Paul shows – a love which puts the welfare and the growth of others in front of his own. How much do we care about the pain of others? How much do we want to see them become mature, stable people who can cope with the pressure of life? And what are we prepared to do to help?

Even within the church there is little evidence that we really want to see others grow. We are more likely to want them to become like us than to become mature people in their own right. And we tend to pray for one another only in times of crisis. But if we are meant to be changing the whole time, should we not pray regularly for one another's spiritual growth?

This will be demanding. It may well mean going beyond praying *for* – sometimes we shall have to pray *with* others. This may mean offering support, encouragement, sympathy or even, on occasions, challenge. It will take time. It will drain our emotional energy and spiritual resources. But the love we are called to show is not some vague, warm emotion. It is the sort of love that will make sacrifices for others, just as Jesus did for us.

Summing it up

> Since, then, you have been raised with Christ, set your hearts on things above, where Christ is seated at the right hand of God. Set your minds on things above, not on earthly things. For you died, and your life is now hidden with Christ in God. When Christ, who is your life, appears, then you also will appear with him in glory. *Colossians 2:1–3*

This is the amazing reality. When Jesus died we died with him and when he was raised we were raised with him. This is why we can confidently expect to live a new, changed life. Our new life is his life. He lives through us and the power and the energy come from him. He is our life. And because of the relationship we have with him we have something to look forward to. I recently watched a television replay of Linford Christie winning the 100 metres in the 1992 Olympics. His eyes were firmly fixed on the tape and all his energies were directed at getting there as fast as possible. It appeared that he could see nothing else. This is the way in which we need to set our minds on Christ. As we do so, our patterns of behaviour will change. But that is another subject and one for the next chapter.

7

LIVING
IN THE
DARKNESS

You've seen the cartoons – a large sign saying 'No Fishing' with someone sitting against it, fishing rod in hand, line in the water. It captures our attitude to rules: 'They're only there to be broken,' a friend of mine used to say in our more rebellious days. It also captures our inconsistency. I remember in 1967 witnessing an anti-Vietnam war demonstration outside the American Embassy in Grosvenor Square. I watched a demonstrator use a large placard inscribed with the single word 'PEACE' to hit a policeman over the head.

God is looking for holy people and, as we have seen, holiness is primarily a matter of relationship with him rather than a matter of obeying rules. There are, however, a lot of rules in the Bible, and indeed in Paul's letters. He often spends the first part of a letter writing about doctrine – the things we should believe – and the second part writing about the way we should behave.

If holiness is about relationship, why the rules? Because no relationship can work unless those involved have some idea of what is expected of them. Rules give us a framework within which a relationship can be worked out.

Belief and behaviour are very closely linked. The Church has been better at working out what it believes than living in ways that are genuinely distinctive. This is unfortunate because it is through our behaviour that we can make a major impact. Jesus calls us to be lights in a dark world (Matthew 5:16). Elsewhere Paul challenges us to 'become blameless and pure, children of God without fault in a crooked and depraved generation', in which we 'shine like stars in the universe' (Philippians 2:15).

What's the problem?

Our world is in a mess and desperately needs to know that there is another way. It is a world of violence on both a national and a personal scale, of discrimination and hatred, of exploitation and oppression. Tragically Christianity is often identified, at least in the popular mind, with violence – as in Northern Ireland; with oppression – as in many parts of Latin America; and with exploitation. The spread of the gospel has brought with it entrepreneurs who have raided the resources of new countries for personal profit and have put little back. These are the perceptions. They are not always accurate but there is enough truth in them to warn us that all is not well. There is a clear challenge. If we want the world to believe that the gospel is of any worth, we have to demonstrate that it changes lives and changes values.

Jesus died to produce a holy people:

> . . . but now he has reconciled you by Christ's
> physical body through death to present you holy in
> his sight. . .
> *Colossians 1:22*

Any idea that salvation is something which gives us a bit of security now and guarantees a blissful eternity for us misses the point. Certainly Jesus died to save us – but salvation and holiness go together. We cannot have one without the other: Those who try to – and there are many who do – haven't really understood the meaning of the cross.

When God made the world, and particularly when he made men and women, he intended that creation should display something of his character. As we know this all went wrong. Men and women thought that they knew better than God; humanity went its own way and failed to live as he intended. However, God determined that, in a corrupt, self-seeking world there would be some at least who stood for him. Noah was the first in a line of godly men that carried on through Abraham and his descendants. When God delivered the Israelites from Egypt it was to make them a holy people (Exodus 19:6). The rest of the Old Testament is the story of their failure to be that people.

God is still determined that his character will be seen in the world and that it will be seen through men and women made in his own image. So he comes, in the Person of his Son Jesus, to redeem and restore confused humanity and make it what it should be.

Holiness is one of those words that frequently gets

misunderstood – and that's one reason why the idea gets a bad press. Holiness is thought of as something negative. Holy people are deadly, boring, killjoys. You won't find them at parties and they don't know any good jokes. They are always looking down their noses, making others feel inferior. In fact they're just the sort of people the rest of us avoid.

But are we missing the point? Who was the holiest person who walked this earth? Jesus. And did he behave like this? No. He was the centre of attraction. He knew how to enjoy a party. When the Pharisees described him as a drinker and glutton they were exaggerating, but there would have been no point in accusing him of being such things unless he knew how to enjoy good food. Jesus accepted people whom others wrote off. He forgave notorious sinners and then spent his time with them. This is what holiness looks like! So let us lay to rest the idea that holy people are negative people. They are positive people who can affirm the good things of life, see them as coming from God, and receive them with thanksgiving (1 Timothy 4:4).

Set apart

The idea behind the Hebrew word for holy is that of being set apart. God is described as holy. This means that his being and his character are completely different from ours. The term holy is also applied to anything that was dedicated to the service of God – set apart for him. The bowls and jars in the temple were described as holy. Because they were designed for God's use they needed to be kept clean, and that meant being kept away from anything that would contaminate them.

When people are described as holy it means that they are set apart for God in a similar way. They live in ways that keep them clean and ready to serve him.

The trouble is that the idea of being kept clear of contamination has become the predominant one. People have lost sight of the great truth that holy people are those who are set apart for God – they have become those who are separated from other things. Holiness, therefore has come to be described in terms of negatives rather than positives. The time has come to reclaim the word.

To be holy is to share the character of God. God made this world of beauty – to be holy is to share God's love of beauty and his enjoyment of his world. God enjoys relationships – to be holy is to value other people and the time we spend with them. Let's see how this works out for Paul.

Time to get changed

> Put to death, therefore, whatever belongs to your
> earthly nature: sexual immorality, impurity, lust,
> evil desires and greed, which is idolatry. Because of
> these, the wrath of God is coming [on those who
> are disobedient]. You used to walk in these ways, in
> the life you once lived. But now you must rid
> yourselves of all such things as these: anger, rage,
> malice, slander and filthy language from your lips.
> Do not lie to each other, since you have taken off
> your old self with its practices and have put on the
> new self, which is being renewed in knowledge in
> the image of its Creator. Here there is no Greek or
> Jew, circumcised or uncircumcised, barbarian,

Scythian, slave or free, but Christ is all, and is in all.
Colossians 3:5–11

So it really is negative after all? No. But change is necessary. If we were invited to a Buckingham Palace garden party we wouldn't complain about having to wear a decent set of clothes. It might even be part of the fun, as we spent time planning the outfit, going round the shops, trying on this and that to get the final effect. Here we are invited into the company of the King of kings and we see getting a new set of clothes as negative?

We do not need to spend too long looking at the things that have to go – we can see enough of them any day, and it's better to spend time with the positives. But there are three things worth noticing. First, Paul is concerned about sexual sin. He does not make it the unforgivable sin, but he does see it as sin. In a society which is saturated with sex we need to hear this. Too many Christians, many in positions of leadership, have destroyed their ministry and damaged others because they have failed in this area. Christians have a reputation for being negatively obsessed with sex and we don't want to foster that. Nor do we want to be harsh with those who fail. But we do want to be aware of the dangers and demonstrate to the world a positive, healthy view of human sexuality.

A world which sees sex as a matter of personal gratification, as a way of establishing one's place in the pecking order, or as a way of financial gain, needs to know that this is not the whole story. It should be told – and shown – by Christians that there is another and better way. That sex is good and enjoyable, but that it is not all there is in life.

In talking of impurity and lust Paul reminds us that it is not simply the activity that matters. He emphasises Jesus' teaching: 'anyone who looks at a woman lustfully (and had he been speaking in the age of the Chippendales he would no doubt have added man) has already committed adultery with her in his heart' (Matthew 5:28). The thought is conceived and nurtured in the privacy of our own minds long before any action takes place. In 1988 the American magazine *Christianity Today* published an article telling the story of one Christian leader's slow decline from soft-pornographic magazines to the sleazy world of peep shows. He tells how he went to consult another respected Christian leader looking for understanding and forgiveness only to find that the second man had gone further down the road and, as a result of his promiscuous activity, was now infected with a range of sexually transmitted diseases. The article led to a flood of correspondence from others who had faced the same struggle. Few of us can claim to be free of lust. But to give into it debases one of the most beautiful aspects of God's creation, degrades other people, damages our relationship with God, and leaves us riddled with guilt.

We who struggle might wish that Paul had given us clearer instructions as to exactly how we are to 'put to death our earthly nature'. It sounds simple expressed like this, but our eyes so easily stray to the top shelf of the newsagents or to the questionable titles in the video store. Paul does give us practical help in coping with lust, but before we look at this, let's note two other points about the things that we must put off.

Take a look at the rather startling mention of greed

– another sin which is characteristic of our consumer-oriented society. See how Paul describes it – as idolatry! Our tendency would be to feel that perhaps it wasn't too serious. But for Paul, to be greedy is to do no less than rob God of his proper place in our lives. The Western world is addicted to possessions, or it was before the present recession began to bite – remember the credit card advert, 'Takes the waiting out of wanting'? Even now, for those in work who have the money, there is still the pressure to have and to consume. This makes it harder still for those who do not have, whether our neighbours or those from other parts of the world. And it leads to crippling debt problems for many.

Just as our world needs to be delivered from its bondage to sex so it needs to be delivered from its bondage to possessions. The early religious orders used to take a vow of chastity, poverty and obedience. They realised that money, sex and power, to use the title of Richard Foster's book, were the trinity of temptations that could wreak havoc with their wellbeing. What we see happening today is the result of indulgence in all three. But while the world cries out for a different way, we Christians show in our own actions all too much the same weakness.

The third thing to note is that so many of these negative qualities are about bad relationships. Our lifestyle is not developed only in the solitude of our own rooms and our own minds but through the rough and tumble of relationships with others. It is here, among those who rub us up the wrong way, whose patterns of behaviour are so different to ours, whose attitudes, whose speech we find difficult, that we really discover how far God's work in us has gone – and how much he still has to do. We'll see a little more of that when we get into the next section.

A new suit

There is a need to change. If, however, we are honest we find change difficult. There are things within us that we hate and long to be rid of, attitudes, thoughts, behavioural patterns that we struggle with but find that we cannot break. It may be some consolation to know that Paul struggled too.

> For what I do is not the good I want to do; no, the evil I do not want to do – this I keep on doing.
>
> *Romans 7:19*

So when he writes about putting off some of the old attitudes, he isn't writing in a vacuum, he is writing from his own personal experience. He probably didn't have all the answers either. But he knows one thing. There is no point in taking off the old clothes unless there is something new to put on in their place.

So we put on the new nature. Our first reaction is to assume that this means great effort on our part – that we have to struggle to change from the people we are. But look again. What we put on is something that God has prepared for us. Paul uses one active verb, 'put on', which is our part, and one passive verb, 'being renewed', which is God's. We cannot create a new nature for ourselves however much we might want to. Only God can do that. But he is not going to force us to do things that we don't want to do. This process of change is a cooperative one. God has his part and we have ours. The harder part is God's. He takes the initiative. All he looks for from us is the willingness to accept what he is doing.

Paul then goes on to spell out what this new nature looks like.

> Therefore, as God's chosen people, holy and dearly loved, clothe yourselves with compassion, kindness, humility, gentleness and patience. Bear with each other and forgive whatever grievances you may have against one another. Forgive as the Lord forgave you. And over all these virtues put on love, which binds them all together in perfect unity. Let the peace of Christ rule in your hearts, since as members of one body you were called to peace. And be thankful. Let the word of Christ dwell in you richly as you teach and admonish one another with all wisdom, and as you sing psalms, hymns and spiritual songs with gratitude in your hearts to God. And whatever you do, whether in word or deed, do it all in the name of the Lord Jesus, giving thanks to God the Father through him. *Colossians 3:12–17*

Paul isn't aiming to make us feel guilty, but to give us something specific to aim for. When we see some of these qualities growing in our lives we can be confident that God is changing us. Notice how the list overlaps with the fruits of the Spirit in Galatians 5:22, 23. This serves as a further reminder that this is God's work and not ours. But we do have to want to be different. We show this by watching our attitudes and our behaviour, rejoicing when we see moves in the right direction, holding back when we find that things are going wrong and expressing our concern over the lack of progress we are bound to feel from time to time.

These good qualities, like the negative ones, are about relationships. Christian lifestyle is not simply, or even primarily, a matter of personal morality. It is a matter of living in relationship with others, and of demonstrating Christlikeness there.

We are to show compassion. The Greek work is a strong one. It implies that when we see others in need we will feel compelled to get out there and do something. Jesus demonstrates this attitude when he sees crowds without food (Matthew 15:32) and without leadership (Matthew 9:36) and when he reaches out and touches lepers (Mark 1:40–55). It is easy to become blasé about the suffering in our world. There is too much of it. Night after night it reaches into the cosy comfort of our living rooms, real and yet somehow unreal. It's all too big. What can we do about it?

We can start where we are. Here it is the church Paul has in mind. He is not writing about the wider world, important though that is. He is urging us, first of all, to show the quality of compassion to those to whom we are closest – those within our own church fellowship. This may be toughest of all! We know one another too well – we have to live alongside one another. Unfortunately, as John makes clear, our attitudes to our fellow Christians are an indication of our relationship with God:

> If anyone has material possessions and sees his
> brother in need but has no pity on him, how can
> the love of God be in him?   *1 John 3:17*

If compassion is hard, kindness can be even harder. It demands that we are always thinking of the needs of others and that we consider their interests. It requires that we encourage them. It prohibits the criticism that so weakens the church of Jesus. We may find others difficult, believe that they don't want to receive kindness, or doubt whether they deserve it (look what he did to me!). But that is not the issue. Nor is it the attitude of Jesus. Remember that what we are aiming to do is to show his character in our own lives.

It gets harder. We are to show humility. We are to 'consider others better than ourselves' (Philippians 2:3). This cuts across the spirit of our age, it upsets the everyday values of the world. Humility is badly misunderstood. It is not an attitude which puts us down – it is an attitude which lifts others up. There is a place for recognising our own unworthiness, but some Christians have made an art-form out of this and ended up with no sense of self-worth or value. I was recently asked to pray with someone for healing. Over a period we saw some improvement. But every time there was a relapse the question was, 'What have I done?' The assumption was that wrong behaviour lay at the root of the sickness. This low self-esteem is not humility. Humility consists in not pushing ourselves forward, in not insisting on our own way. The best picture of humility is Jesus who takes for himself the description of the servant in Isaiah:

> Here is my servant whom I have chosen,
>   the one I love, in whom I delight;
> I will put my Spirit on him,
>   and he will proclaim justice to the nations.
> He will not quarrel or cry out;
>   no-one will hear his voice in the streets.
> A bruised reed he will not break,

> and a smouldering wick he will not snuff out,
> till he leads justice to victory.
> In his name the nations will put their hope.
>
> *Matthew 12:18–21*

Gentleness conjures up the picture of a mother with a child. Harsh words and actions are ruled out. If we recognise the weakness and vulnerability of others, we will avoid those harsh words and actions which might cause damage. Yes, there will be times when we have to deal with issues in the life of the church or of another Christian which require firmness. But it is possible to be gentle and firm. Too often firmness is confused with harshness. Heavy approaches to church discipline do more damage than good. The aim of discipline is to restore gently (Galatians 6:1).

This will help us to be patient, too. When Peter came and asked Jesus how often he should forgive, he was revealing the same lack of patience that we so often show to one another. We become irritated with people when they do not seem to understand things, or when they continually make demands on us. Look at Jesus again. Confronted by disciples who were slow to understand, he patiently repeated his teaching again and again hoping that light would dawn.

Our patience is most readily seen in terms of our ability to forgive. Failure to forgive is probably one of the most destructive elements in the life of today's church. There are churches where people will not talk to one another because of incidents way back in the past, where husband and wife have fallen out and sit on opposite sides of the church, where church meetings are marked by disagreements which took place years earlier. Lack of forgiveness is infectious and it spreads like a cancer. It denies the fundamentals of the gospel. God sent Jesus into the world so that we could be forgiven, and our failure to forgive shows that we have not understood this. Instead of being forgiven, we are in danger of losing our forgiveness. Could this be? Surely God cannot take away the forgiveness he offers? Jesus says he can and he will (Matthew 6:15). Paul puts it the other way round, urging us to forgive because we have been forgiven by God. In practice, as we understand the values of the forgiveness God offers us, we forgive others and then experience more of God's forgiveness.

Underlying all these qualities is love. Not the romantic, misty-eyed emotion of modern imagination, still less the self-centred sexual gratification that goes under the same name, but love as an act of the will, a decision to care for another, to put him or her first. Sometimes love is not a matter of how we feel, but a determination to have the mind of Jesus (Philippians 2:1–5). We are not to show love only to those whom we find attractive but to all. Love does not ask what it can get but what it can give. There is no better description of it than in the well-known verses of 1 Corinthians 13. And there is no better example of it than that to be found in the life of Jesus who gave his time and his energy to outcasts, to prostitutes, to those on the margins of society, to those without power or influence in the world. When we begin to act like Jesus did, we begin to understand love. It is hardly surprising that all the other qualities we have discussed – gentleness, patience, forgiveness – have their root in love. It unites them, drives them, and provides the soil in which they can grow.

Love can only exist in community. The man on a desert island can claim to love others but his claim can never be tested. Only when he leaves the island and enters into relationships can he experience or demonstrate love. There is a risk involved. People are not things; they have minds of their own, they are delightfully unpredictable, and loving them involves risking rejection. It means putting ourselves on the line, sharing something of what we are, knowing that others will not always understand. Offering them ourselves, knowing that they may not want us. This is the path that Jesus trod and there is no other way. So Paul takes us back to the idea of community, worked out in three different ways.

The church

> Let the peace of Christ rule in your hearts, since as
> members of one body you were called to peace.
> And be thankful. Let the word of Christ dwell in you
> richly as you teach and admonish one another with
> all wisdom, and as you sing psalms, hymns and
> spiritual songs with gratitude in your hearts to God.
> And whatever you do, whether in word or deed, do
> it all in the name of the Lord Jesus, giving thanks
> to God the Father through him.   *Colossians 3:15–17*

The first phrase here has been misquoted and misunderstood. Time and time again we hear peace referred to as an individual thing. Often it is seen in terms of guidance or freedom from worry. That is not Paul's point. He is writing about harmony within the church and community. Here lies the true test of the depth of

132

Christ's work in our lives. While we squabble and disagree, while our church meetings are marked by self-interest, while we divide over absurdly small matters of doctrine which depend only on our personal interpretation, we fail to show the life of Christ within us. The world is without Christ. Hence its violence. We can model a different way, a way of peace. But we can hardly join the protests about world aggression while we cannot agree among ourselves.

Our lives together are to be marked by thankfulness. In the midst of a greedy and grasping world, a world which so often complains, we demonstrate a spirit of gratitude. This sets us free from our captivity to material things because it enables us to see them not as a right but as a good gift from God. The practice of giving thanks before food has declined in Christian circles and there is no value in doing this simply as some sort of ritual. But it would be a pity to lose the opportunity which giving thanks provides to acknowledge our dependence on the goodness of a creator God. Our gratitude must be genuine. I remember receiving an envelope from a Christian publisher. It was postmarked 'Gratitude's the attitude, Praise the Lord!' Twee, I thought, but a worthy sentiment. Unfortunately, the letter proceeded to rebuke me at great length for my alleged failure to abide by the small print of a copyright agreement and to threaten legal action should I not comply immediately. Not much real thankfulness there!

If we can receive all that comes with a sense of gratitude it will take the sting out of those things that create disunity. But even as I write I know how far short I fall in this area. As I sit in the morning worship, can I receive the dreadful guitar playing, or the whining self-centred praying with thanks or do I allow it to make me negative and jaundiced? I know what I should do, I know what Christ would have done – and I know what I actually do! We all have some way to go on these things.

Our thankfulness will show itself in our worship. Paul has two key things to say about worship here. It is centred on the word of Christ and it is an expression of the living life of the community. There is a tendency for worship to be self-indulgent. Obviously the style in which we worship reflects our personality and our Christian experience. There is nothing wrong with this. But if it is shaped only by our personal preferences, if we only do those things that we enjoy, we have not understood its true nature. Worship should bring God glory. To do so it needs shape and direction. It needs to have, at its heart, something which is true, something on which to rely, something which reminds us of the nature and character of God. This is what Paul has in mind when he encourages the Colossians to have the word of Christ dwelling in them.

This is the strength of liturgical forms of worship which have readings from Scripture at their heart. It can also be a feature of more spontaneous forms of worship in which the Spirit leads individuals to particular passages of Scripture. Paul seems to have had something like this in mind. Whatever the form, it is only when we have taken the Word into our hearts and minds that it can emerge and stimulate our worship.

Worship is something in which all participate. Paul seems to envisage a pattern in which during the worship a variety of individuals have the opportunity to speak under the inspiration of the Spirit. This was the norm in Corinth and there seems no reason why Colossae should have been any different. Of course, we do not have to adopt identical patterns. There are different patterns in Scripture. We should, however, look for forms of worship which give freedom to all and which recognise that all have the opportunity to hear God and respond to him. Above all we should worship in a way which enables us to focus on the character and activity of God.

Worship should grow out of our life together, and reflect our concerns and those of our community. The popular idea that when we enter a church building we leave the world behind and come into the presence of God is unfortunate. When we come to God we bring ourselves, our feelings and our concerns with us. The world is part of our concern; it is part of God's concern. Worship concentrates our attention on God and his glory. But how can we honour God if we ignore the world he made and cares for? Worship gives us the opportunity to see the world and its needs in the light of God's character and then, with fresh understanding, new vision and clearer purpose, to go back to that world as God's agents of change. When our exposition of Scripture, our prayers, our songs, our words of prophecy engage with the issues of the day, we will hear God speak, find ourselves lifted and be better equipped to serve him.

On the home front

> Wives, submit to your husbands, as is fitting in the
> Lord. Husbands, love your wives and do not be
> harsh with them. Children, obey your parents in
> everything, for this pleases the Lord. Fathers, do
> not embitter your children, or they will become
> discouraged. *Colossians 3:18–21*

Relationships in the home are among the hardest to get
right. They are also among the most revealing. In a
parallel passage in Ephesians 5:21, Paul starts off by
reminding his readers that we are to submit to one
another. This is not a question of one party being
superior to the other, a charter for husbands to treat
their wives as slaves who must obey their every whim
or for parents to see children merely as status symbols.
It describes a new pattern for family life which sees
each member as having equal status and equal rights.
There are differences of role which will be worked out
in varying ways depending on the society in which we
live. Family life in the western societies of the twentieth
century is very different to that of first century Colossae.
We have to work out for ourselves what the practical
implications of the principles might be. There is room
for different patterns of family life; we cannot insist
that there is only one Christian way of organising a
family.

The key to getting it right is the conviction that
each person matters. We are not to insist on our own
rights but to ensure that those of others are protected.
Too often husbands have seen the instruction to wives
to submit as something which gives them rights over
their wives. Such husbands are, in fact, directly disobey-

ing the command to love their wives. It is interesting that in the parallel passage in Ephesians 5:21 the encouragement to wives to submit follows directly from the words 'Submit to one another'. Wives and husbands have to work out together what submission means today. Paul's words oppose both slavish obedience and aggressive demands. Submission is not primarily an issue of women's right or of feminism, although we cannot ignore these things as part of our contemporary context. It is an issue of mutual love and respect.

In an age when half of all marriages contracted will end in divorce, Christians can show that there is another way. This is part and parcel of confronting the darkness. But too often we have been part of the darkness ourselves, either by conforming to the standards of our society or by setting up an alternative which owes more to patterns of male domination than to the liberating gospel of Jesus Christ.

Much the same is true of relationships with our children. In recent years we have seen lurid stories of sexual abuse and renewed emphasis on child safety. While some of the stories may have been exaggerated by a sensation-seeking press, child abuse is far more common than we realise. Most ministers and counsellors will have come across people well into adult life who have been the victims of physical or sexual abuse, sometimes at the hands of Christian parents, some of whom have held positions of authority within the church. If we are going to address the problem, we will need to put a new emphasis on the value of children and combine this with a greater awareness of the problem, a refusal to sweep it under the carpet and a willingness to provide more support for those under pressure. Then there will be new hope.

Working practices

Paul's final concern is the workplace. Here our culture makes his illustration even more alien to us. We live in an age when contracts of employment are required by law and organised labour has the power to close down companies:

> Slaves, obey your earthly masters in everything; and do it, not only when their eye is on you and to win their favour, but with sincerity of heart and reverence for the Lord. Whatever you do, work at it with all your heart, as working for the Lord, not for men, since you know that you will receive an inheritance from the Lord as a reward. It is the Lord Christ you are serving. Anyone who does wrong will be repaid for his wrong, and there is no favouritism. Masters, provide your slaves with what is right and fair, because you know that you also have a Master in heaven.   *Colossians 3:22–4:1*

There are principles which we can still apply to our changed scene. Justice is necessary – and market forces do not always make for justice. Employers need to beware of simply going along with accepted practice. How fair and right are large pay differentials? How fair is it for one person to work long hours and another to do the minimum? How fair are some of the conditions in which we ask our employees to work? And employees have a range of questions too. Is trying to get away with the minimum amount of work really doing whatever we do with all our heart? Would we be playing computer games in the middle of the afternoon if we really believed that we were doing our work for God?

The truly revolutionary thing about Paul's teaching here is that employer and employee alike stand under God. Each is called to his or her role by God. Neither makes up the rules of the game; each is called to play by God's rules. In a society where work is seen as the ultimate mark of an individual's worth, we can emphasise that work is good because it is God-given, while pointing out that it can be corrupted and used for selfish ends. For many people work is seen as boring, but as necessary in order to live. We may have to encourage some new thinking which sees work not in terms of paid employment but in terms of creative activity. Those who remain at home rearing children or caring for older relatives are making a useful contribution to the life of the community. So are those involved in voluntary work. The key indicator should not be how much we earn, but how much God is glorified and humanity benefited by what we do. If we can help people to see things in this way, we may begin a revolution which the darkness will not be able to withstand. This is what God asks of us.

Cleaning the lens

When I was a child we used to take an annual holiday in Felixstowe. Six miles off the coast was the Cork lightship and in the evenings we would sit on the beach and watch the beam of warning light flash out. Some years we would take a small boat trip out to the lightship and on one occasion we were allowed to stop and look around. In the lamphouse everything was spot-lessly clean. The lens and the mirror can only do their job if they are properly maintained. In this way they are able to act as a warning and save the lives of sailors. Why, in a book on confronting the darkness, has there been a long chapter on Christian lifestyle? Simply because we can only confront the darkness with light, and the only light we have is the light of Christian character. As Paul wrote to the Philippians:

> . . . so that you may become blameless and pure, children of God without fault in a crooked and depraved generation, in which you shine like stars in the universe.   Philippians 2:15

If we are going to bring any light into the surrounding darkness we will have to live in different and distinctive ways. This will not be easy. It will take time and energy. It may make us unpopular. But there is no other way.

8

SENT
INTO THE
DARKNESS

The time has come to draw the threads together.
We have seen Christ as he stands before the world he
made, the world that has deserted him. We have seen
how he calls a people to himself, a new people, a holy
people who will demonstrate his values in our dark
world.

Paul, from the moment he met the risen Lord on
the Damascus road, lived for one great purpose. He had
discovered something, Someone, so momentous that the
news had to be told. The secret of the ages, long hidden,
had now been revealed to him, Paul, the persecutor of
the church and of Jesus himself. This was cause for
celebration. Cause, too, for wanting to bring others in
on the good news.

> Now I rejoice in what was suffered for you, and I
> fill up in my flesh what is still lacking in regard to

Christ's afflictions, for the sake of his body, which is the church. I have become its servant by the commission God gave me to present to you the word of God in its fulness – the mystery that has been kept hidden for ages and generations, but is now disclosed to the saints. To them God has chosen to make known among the Gentiles the glorious riches of this mystery, which is Christ in you, the hope of glory. We proclaim him, admonishing and teaching everyone with all wisdom, so that we may present everyone perfect in Christ. To this end I labour, struggling with all his energy, which so powerfully works in me. I want you to know how much I am struggling for you and for those at Laodicea, and for all who have not met me personally.

Colossians 1:24–2:1

Paul is the servant of the church; he is also God's servant. Some of us find it easy enough to be God's servants. We do as we believe he wants, we gain pleasure and satisfaction from serving him, but ask us to work for our fellow Christians, to submit to their wishes or care for their interests, and that is a different matter. We need to do both. In fact we need one another to make sure that we are doing what God wants. Just as we cannot love God unless we also love one another (1 John 4:20, 21) so we cannot serve God unless we serve one another.

We serve God, we serve his church and we serve the world. We are under an obligation to let others in on the secret, to give them the hope of glory. This, for Paul, was his life's work. He never for one moment imagined that he would ever be able to give up. He was under a compulsion:

> Yet when I preach the gospel, I cannot boast, for I
> am compelled to preach. Woe to me if I do not
> preach the gospel!   *1 Corinthians 9:16*

It is as though some modern researcher has found a cure for AIDS or malaria. She has the answer to the need of many suffering people and can't keep the news to herself. It must be shared. We have discovered something which will bring relief to those suffering from sin. We can hardly keep such momentous news to ourselves.

The idea that sharing the good news is one thing and helping people to become mature disciples another is a modern invention. Paul wouldn't have recognised it. When he went into a town he started by telling people about Jesus. As some became Christians he told them more. The process of learning took several months. He then appointed leaders in the church and moved on. It is unhelpful to draw a line between evangelism and teaching, between making converts and making disciples. The goal of evangelism is not conversion but maturity. In practice we find that evangelism involves teaching and that teaching can lead to conversion.

All involved

Lest we should think that evangelism is something for experts like Paul or Billy Graham, Paul has a word for us.

> Be wise in the way you act towards outsiders; make
> the most of every opportunity. Let your
> conversation be always full of grace, seasoned with
> salt, so that you may know how to answer everyone.
> *Colossians 4:5, 6*

He is looking for something natural. We think of evangelism as something special or different, something we turn on. This was the sort of thing that Becky Pippert was thinking of when she said, 'Evangelism is something you wouldn't do to your dog.' We imagine people going round with glazed eyes and messages like, 'Repent, the end is nigh.' But this wasn't what Paul had in mind, nor was it how the early church behaved. For them their Christian faith was as much a part of their lives as the food they ate, the clothes they wore, the things they did. Wherever they went they spoke about it naturally and easily.

In other words these early Christians were driven by deep concerns to share what they had discovered. But they were driven not only by their understanding of the gospel but also by their understanding of the world. The key is found in verses that we have already looked at:

> ... who has qualified you to share in the inheritance
> of the saints in the kingdom of light. For he has
> rescued us from the dominion of darkness and
> brought us into the kingdom of the Son he loves ...
> *Colossians 1:12, 13*

For these Christians there was a clear divide. Satan ruled the world, a world inhabited by malevolent forces, which held people captive, causing distress and illness, creating fear. This was the dominion of darkness and it left people hopeless (Ephesians 2:12). It is hard for us to imagine today. Our world has its fears but they come in different forms. It experiences hopelessness but for many of us this is rather remote. We talk glibly about how miserable non-Christians are, but often they are perfectly happy. We paint a bleak picture of the horrors of being without Christ. But while it may be true in the abstract that life without Christ is meaningless, this is not everyone's experience. We need to find some new description of the situation of those who have not found Christ which relates to the world we know, the post-Christian, post-modern world in which anything goes. We know that people are lost and have an uncertain future, but while this occurs to many of the less fortunate in society, there are others for whom it is far from obvious.

Maybe the clue ultimately lies in the uncertainty and insecurity of our world. Those things have become more manifest since the stock markets of the western world collapsed together in 1987. The recession has left record numbers unemployed, houses have been repossessed at rates not seen before (at least in Britain), and great difficulties have surrounded the emergence of the new states in Eastern Europe, with fears that further conflict might draw others in. The uncertainty created by the bomb in the sixties and seventies has now been replaced by economic uncertainty. If these are the fears of our age, created by the worship of the golden gods of materialism, then perhaps bringing Christ's message to bear on them is a good place to start.

Back, however, to the early Church. Their understanding of the nature of the world enabled them to see just how big was the change that Jesus had made. Their goal was to see others freed from the powers that held them captive to enjoy new life in Christ. We shall only understand their motivation when we see that, in our world just as much as in theirs, Christ makes a difference.

It is also important to understand the nature of this kingdom that we have been brought into. When we hear the word kingdom we think of a physical location, but the Bible speaks more in terms of the active rule of God. To come into the kingdom of his Son is to come under the rule of his Son, to recognise him as Lord and King. This introduces another important truth. The Kingdom is not the Church. It is wider than the church. God rules over the whole of his creation and over all people. The kingdom of darkness may be real but it only has partial and temporary power. As we have seen Jesus has brought about its final defeat. The Church exists as a witness to the present and future rule of God. It shows what that rule will look like or, at least, it should. It invites others to share that rule.

Jesus' message was that the kingdom had come – that is our message too. We are called to make others aware of the presence of the kingdom as God works through us. We can do this through our words and through our actions. Jesus and the early church always supported what they said by actions. Sometimes it was signs and wonders which demonstrated the presence of the kingdom. Sometimes it was getting alongside outcasts and showing them love. The kingdom is still seen wherever a cup of water is offered in Jesus' name, wherever the good news is proclaimed and wherever healing or deliverance take place under the authority of Jesus. One of the great tragedies of our time is that most of us find the kingdom in one or two of these things but not in all three. Those who have majored on proclamation have spurned the charismatics, the charismatics have felt that those who had a vision for social action had no gospel, the social activists have assumed that the rest do not care and so on. This is because we have not understood the all-encompassing nature of the kingdom.

Life and word

Paul's understanding of the kingdom helps us see that mission is more complex than we might have thought. There are two major elements. Our lifestyle matters. It is no coincidence that the verses with which we started this chapter follow Paul's teaching about the way Christians should live. If we are going to make any impact on the futility and insecurity of our world, our lives will have to demonstrate that what we believe really does make a difference. Our convictions have to be carried through into the small affairs of every day. A minister I know tells of overhearing one of his congregation talking with a non-Christian friend in a bus queue. Both were complaining bitterly about the weather. What a difference, he says, it would have made if the Christian could have taken a more positive view, if somehow her Christian faith had made a difference to the way she thought about something as mundane as the weather.

Against the disillusionment and pain of failed relationships we have to show that relationships can survive and bring joy and fulfilment. Against the lies that characterise so much of business and personal relationships we must demonstrate that there are people of integrity. A friend told me the story of someone who was responsible for packing the finished articles in a glass factory. Articles that came off the production line damaged were treated in one way, articles broken in packing had to be treated in another. It was accepted practice to treat both damaged and broken items as 'damaged in manufacture' (as I recall there were insurance implications). When the packer became a Christian she stood out against this, believing that the truth mattered. Because she refused to go along with the established way of doing things she eventually lost her job. Another friend found it necessary to leave a satisfying and well-paid job simply because he felt that certain practices within the company didn't square with his Christian principles.

We need more people like these – people who are prepared to be different even when it costs. They will not always be popular. The central problem for the early Christians was that recognising Christ as Lord brought them into immediate conflict with the authorities. The Roman system demanded, at least towards the end of the first century, that Caesar be acknowledged as Lord and the custom was to burn incense to him. Christians could not compromise their faith in this way and as a result many died.

Polycarp was bishop of Smyrna in the middle of the second century. Discovered hiding in a farm during a period of persecution, he received the officers courteously and asked for time to pray. After praying for two hours he was brought before the magistrate. 'Swear the oath,' said the magistrate, 'and I will release you.' Polycarp replied, 'I have served him for eighty-six years and he has never wronged me; how can I blaspheme my King and Saviour?' Polycarp was burnt at the stake. Perpetua was a young mother of twenty-two. Begged by her father and the governor to offer sacrifice to the Roman emperor she refused. She was thrown to the lions.

Paul gives special attention to our conversation. And this, as we know, is where we are so often let down. How often have we let something slip only to regret it almost immediately. Gossip and back-biting have probably damaged the cause of Christianity more than anything else. We need to beware of negative and careless talk. Our conversation needs positive qualities. To talk of it being seasoned is apt. Food without seasoning is flat and unappetising. Our conversation should be interesting and have an edge. It should relate to the issues of our world but bring a Christian perspective. Unfortunately Christians have gained the reputation of being boring. Sometimes this is because, rightly, they will not take part in all the activities which non-Christians regard as essential. But sometimes it is, quite frankly, because we have nothing to talk about which will interest our contemporaries. We have become so involved in our own closed world that we have no points of contact. Those who are wise live both in the world of their contemporary culture and the world of the gospel. We cannot hope to make the truth of Scripture relevant to those with whom we live unless we know something of their world.

In his book *Peace Child*, Don Richardson tells of the great difficulty of making any impact in the headhunting culture of Irian Jaya until he discovered a local custom. A child was exchanged between warring tribes and while the so-called peace child was alive there was peace. When Don Richardson saw the parallels between this and God sending his Son as our peace child, he found a way of making the gospel intelligible. We too need to look for points of contact which will lead to conversation that is seasoned. When we bring a Christian perspective to the events and affairs of our world we build bridges that people can cross to enter the kingdom. The tragedy is that so many of us are, to use an old phrase, so heavenly-minded that we are of no earthly use.

We need more Christians who will go where people are and meet them on their own ground. And we need churches who will understand that if we miss the prayer meeting to go to a football match or the sugarcraft guild with a non-Christian friend, we have a model in the Jesus who went to village weddings and dinner parties with tax collectors! I well remember the summer evening many years ago when I walked round the church car park in silence with a friend as he struggled towards the point of Christian faith. I also remember the many Saturday mornings on the tennis court which had gone before.

Jesus tells us we are the light of the world, the salt of the earth. Too often the light shines only for those who have already experienced its benefits rather than for the weary and the lost. The salt is not allowed to penetrate where its flavouring and preserving qualities are needed. The time has come to break out of our cosy Christian ghettoes and enter the dark places of the world.

Success guaranteed

One of the reasons we give up on evangelism is that we doubt if anything will happen. We have tried and failed – so why try again? True enough success does seem limited. But take a look at the broader picture.

> All over the world this gospel is bearing fruit and growing, just as it has been doing among you since the day you heard it and understood God's grace in all its truth. *Colossians 1:6*

Things are happening today as they were then. In Africa people are becoming Christians at such a rate that some experts envisage the whole of Africa being Christian by early next century. In many parts of Latin America and East Asia too the church is growing rapidly. So the gospel does make its mark. Even in those Western countries that have turned away from Christianity there are places where, against the trend, people are hearing about Jesus and finding that he is good news for them. There is good reason to be confident.

I like the story which Derek Tidball tells of picking up a hitchhiker who asked him in the course of conversation what he did. On discovering that his driver was a minister, the rather nervous response was, 'What does it feel like to be on the losing side?' 'I wouldn't know,' said Derek.

There is, on the other hand, no reason to be complacent – the work still has to be done. And doing it may be something of a struggle. Let's take another look at the verses with which we started this chapter:

> Now I rejoice in what was suffered for you, and I
> fill up in my flesh what is still lacking in regard to
> Christ's afflictions, for the sake of his body, which is
> the church. . . . We proclaim him, admonishing and
> teaching everyone with all wisdom, so that we may
> present everyone perfect in Christ. To this end I
> labour, struggling with all his energy, which so
> powerfully works in me. I want you to know how
> much I am struggling for you and for those at
> Laodicea, and for all who have not met me personally.
> *Colossians 1:24–2:1*

Proclamation is a painful business. Paul knew two sorts
of pain – one which he describes as filling up in his flesh
what was still lacking in regard to Christ's afflictions,
and one which results from struggling for the conversion and discipling of his generation.

The first gives Bible interpreters one of their hardest
tasks. What did Paul mean? Obviously he didn't mean
that Christ's sufferings were somehow incomplete or
ineffective, for that would have gone against all that he
taught (see for example 2:13, 14). We may never find a
complete answer. In part it comes from the very close
relationship between Jesus and his followers. Paul could
hardly have forgotten his own conversion, when he
heard Jesus say, 'Saul, Saul, why do you persecute me?'
Those words would have stayed with him. Reflecting
on their meaning he came to see that for Christians to
suffer was for Jesus to suffer, and for Jesus to suffer
was for Christians to suffer. All the pain that came
Paul's way – the hunger, the beatings, the shipwrecks,
the stonings – came because he was serving Christ.

This first kind of pain also owes something to the
two kingdoms that we looked at. In Jewish thought

the arrival of the kingdom of God was to be heralded by birth pains, natural upheavals, human disagreement, unusual suffering. Some of this comes out in Jesus' own teaching in Mark 13 and Matthew 24 where he speaks of his return. Just as Jesus faced opposition, human and spiritual, in his own ministry, so will we. The coming of the kingdom of God involves struggle. The enemy has been conclusively defeated but there are still, in the words of one theologian, some mopping up operations.

There is pain (of this first sort) too, in seeing the world as Jesus sees it. This is where a vision for mission starts. When Jesus looked at the city of Jerusalem he wept over it. Those who are most effective in telling others about Jesus are those who know what it is to look at lost, broken, hurting humans with Jesus' eyes and weep for them. Once we have begun to feel the world's hurt with Jesus we shall feel compelled to go out and do something about it. This may be through telling how God has shown his love. It may be through showing that love in practical ways.

Paul's second pain came from the sheer hard work of sharing the gospel and caring for others. Anyone who has pastored a church, led a youth group, taken part in a children's mission, been involved in the school or college Christian Union or given themselves to any other form of Christian activity, and done it conscientiously, will know what Paul means. There are days when we do not think we have anything left to give – but the job must still be done. There are times when we feel that if one more person with needs comes our way we shall scream and run a mile and then one does, and we reach for the kettle and the coffee.

Ours is an age of instant results. We want the

satisfaction without any effort. We want our Christian work, our mission, our evangelism, to be like cup-a-soup – complete the moment we add hot water. But evangelism is more like making soup the old fashioned way – finding the ingredients, preparing them properly and cooking them carefully. It takes a lot more time and energy but the results are worth it. There can be benefit in struggle, hard work and even in suffering, however much that cuts across the grain of our easy-going twentieth-century philosophy.

Dietrich Bonhoeffer, the German Pastor killed by the Nazis in 1944 wrote a book called *The Cost of Discipleship*. In it he pointed out that there is no such thing as cheap grace. Forgiveness may be freely offered but there is always a price to pay. Grace cannot be cheap for it cost God the life of his Son. Whenever we suffer in the cause of the gospel we are showing the world that God loves it so much that he too was prepared to suffer.

This is why the thinking to be found among New Age followers, and in some forms of Christianity, which tries to pretend that we are intended to live a pain-free, suffering-free life is so dangerous. Such thinking actually undermines one of the central truths of the gospel. In the end it leaves us with no good news. Why? Because it leaves us with no cross.

Here is the counterbalance to the last section. Yes, the gospel will always triumph. But that does not mean that we can lapse into an easy triumphalism. In May 1940 Winston Churchill, speaking of the struggle with Germany, said to the House of Commons, 'I have nothing to offer but blood, toil, tears and sweat.' Christ would say something similar to us. He has promised us struggle (see Matthew 10:17–25).

Getting on with it

For Paul spreading the gospel was all about partnership. He always travelled with people. On his first trip he had Barnabas and others, for John Mark was clearly included in the party. He later travelled with Silas and there were times when Luke was with them. Probably others joined him from time to time making a larger group. Sometimes they worked alongside Paul, sometimes they went off to do a specific piece of work somewhere else.

Beyond this there was a wider group still. Nearly all Paul's letters contain personal greetings and messages to several individuals. Some readers pass over these, thinking that there is little of value in them compared to the meat of the letters. For those who will look, however, there are important lessons to learn.

> Tychicus will tell you all the news about me. He is a dear brother, a faithful minister and fellow-servant in the Lord. I am sending him to you for the express purpose that you may know about our circumstances and that he may encourage your hearts. He is coming with Onesimus, our faithful and dear brother, who is one of you. They will tell you everything that is happening here. My fellow-prisoner Aristarchus sends you his greetings, as does Mark, the cousin of Barnabas. (You have received instructions about him; if he comes to you, welcome him.) Jesus, who is called Justus, also sends greetings. These are the only Jews among my fellow-workers for the kingdom of God, and they have

proved a comfort to me. Epaphras, who is one of you and a servant of Christ Jesus, sends greetings. He is always wrestling in prayer for you, that you may stand firm in all the will of God, mature and fully assured. I vouch for him that he is working hard for you and for those at Laodicea and Hierapolis. Our dear friend Luke, the doctor, and Demas send greetings. Give my greetings to the brothers at Laodicea, and to Nympha and the church in her house. After this letter has been read to you, see that it is also read in the church of the Laodiceans and that you in turn read the letter from Laodicea. Tell Archippus: 'See to it that you complete the work you have received in the Lord.' I, Paul, write this greeting in my own hand. Remember my chains. Grace be with you.   *Colossians 4:7–18*

What a fascinating list – a whole novel could be woven around these few verses! It would be wonderful to know more about some of the characters who confronted the darkness of the first century, many unknown apart from this brief mention. What a rich social mix they present – from Onesimus the slave to Nympha the householder! The list includes those who have failed – Onesimus the runaway slave now restored to his master through their mutual relationship with Jesus, and Mark, whom we look at below – as well as the success stories. There are men and women for Paul was happy to work alongside both. The idea that he had no time for women just doesn't stand up.

Mark is worth a special mention. He failed, and, it would appear, failed badly on Paul's first missionary journey. Paul was in no mood then to give him another chance. But he must have relented, for here Mark is restored to favour. Paul later describes him as helpful in his ministry (2 Timothy 4:11). Most of us can look back to some failure in our Christian work. Some of us will still be feeling that because of past failure we have nothing to offer in the future. Here is encouragement. No failure can finally disqualify us. We may need a period of restoration, we may have to return to a rather different form of ministry, there will certainly need to be repentance; but there is always the possibility of renewed service. Gordon Macdonald was a well-known writer and the leader of a major Christian organisation in the United States. But there came a point when, through personal failure, his world fell apart and he left the ministry. In his book *Restoring Your Broken World*, he speaks honestly about his own failure and shows the way towards restoration. Peter denied the Lord not once but three times, went out, wept bitterly and then went back to his fishing. But Jesus found him there. Read John 21:14–21 and see how Jesus restores and recommissions him. If you are feeling the effects of your own failure, let Jesus find you where you are and restore you.

Then there is Ephraphas. He knew the suffering that comes from being involved in mission. Formerly he had worked in the church at Colossae; probably the Colossians first heard the gospel through him. He had seen, and rejoiced in, their growth. Now he is with Paul and he expresses his concern in prayer. Paul describes this as working hard! When did we last think of our prayer as hard work? When was it hard work? If we will not struggle at this level we can hardly expect to be successful. All the great forward moves of God have started in prayer, and have continued in prayer. To give up on prayer is to give up. Ephaphras knew it. Do we?

It would be wrong to assume that Paul was always surrounded by friends. There is more than a hint here of personal loneliness. Only three Jews work with him and yet his great longing has always been for his own people. Mission can still be a lonely business. I once met a woman who had spent twenty years as the only European in a North African town. Despite these years of faithful witness she never saw anyone become a Christian. Involvement in mission will not always guarantee us friends. Indeed it may bring us enemies, as Aristarchus, in the passage we have just read, clearly discovered.

But let the last word be with the ordinary people named here who got involved in the mission of the early church. It was they who strode, armed with the light of the gospel into the darkness of the false religions, the occultism, the superstition, the economic collapse, the political uncertainty, the moral failure of the first century. Today, still, it is the ordinary people, the small, the unknown, like ourselves, who will stand against the same pressures and bring light and hope to a dark world at the end of the twentieth century.

> The light shines in the darkness, but the darkness
> has not understood it. *John 1:5*

> You are the light of the world. A city on a hill cannot
> be hidden. Neither do people light a lamp and put
> it under a bowl. Instead they put it on its stand,
> and it gives light to everyone in the house. In the
> same way, let your light shine before men, that they
> may see your good deeds and praise your Father in
> heaven. *Matthew 5:14–16*

OTHER BOOKS IN THE SERIES

Pioneers or Settlers? Exodus: Adventurous faith for today (Philip Mohabir)

Tested by Fire: Daniel 1–6: Solid faith in today's world (Chris Wright)

Hunger for Holiness: Malachi: A call to commitment today (Stephen Gaukroger)

God of New Beginnings: Matthew 1–4 in today's world (Roger Sainsbury)

Thirsty for God: Matthew 5–7: Jesus' teaching for today (Stephen Gaukroger)

Drawing Power: Living out Acts in today's world (Derek Prime)

People Under Pressure: 2 Corinthians: Strategy for stress (Michael Cole)

Open to Others: Ephesians: Overcoming barriers in today's church (Colin Buchanan)

Growing in Christ: 1 Thessalonians: Steps to Christian maturity (Paul Marsh)

Growing Your Gifts: 2 Timothy: Ministry in today's world (Stephen Gaukroger)